The Operalicious Cookbook

by Wayne Line, Baritone

Conceived by Sylvia Volk, Opera Buffs

Edited by Eileen Breen, Nickel City Opera

To the fabulous Kernis-listen and enjoy!

Love —

Eileen

Opera & Food

"Every single opera, at least if it doesn't refer to food, it refers to some sort of passion and that's one of the things people relate to," the soprano Carol Vaness said. "For even Wagner, it's got that 'food of the gods' feeling to it. Opera is about life. How could you describe people's lives without having them eat?" Hardly a performance goes by without some reference to a meal.

Food is so central to the operas of Giuseppe Verdi that the University of Notre Dame musicologist Pierpaolo Polzonetti has written papers on the subject. He came up with what he calls the laws of "gastromusicology" to explain what food can signify in opera. "The first law is that no meal can be sad, no matter what, when people eat, people seem to be happy, even if something bad is going to happen." Other laws hold that meals show social cohesion and that the presence of food or drink "excludes immediate catastrophe" except, as in operas like Simon Boccanegra when poison is involved.

It has been said Verdi used drinking and eating as plot devices. One of the master's most auspicious meals comes in his lesser-known opera buffa, Un giorno di regno (King for a Day), with a chorus of waiters and diners attending a "sumptuous banquet" at the start of the opera.

The title character of Verdi's Falstaff is known as one of the great operatic eaters. His bill at the Garter Inn, as he recounts at the opera's opening, is for 6 chickens, 3 turkeys, 2 pheasants, 1 anchovy and 30 bottles of sherry. In Macbeth, Verdi prescribes a "sumptuously prepared feast" for the banquet scene when Banquo's ghost appears.

Puccini also included meal in his operas, particularly *La Boheme* a story of starving artists in 19th-century Paris. In their chilly garret on Christmas Eve, Rodolfo, Schaunard, Colline and Marcello dine on a cold roast, Bordeaux and pastry. Later, at Café Momus in the Latin Quarter, they order sausage, roast venison, turkey, Rhine wine and lobster and eat "*a poem*" of a chicken, as Colline sings. Outside vendors hawk Parisian street food; oranges, dates, hot chestnuts, nougat, whipped cream, candies, fruit tarts, coconut milk, carrots, trout and plums. A sumptuous evening in contrast to their friend Mimi's consumptive and tragic death.

In Humperdinck's Hansel and Gretel, the witch invites the unsuspecting hungry children into her house for a fattening up before consumption. She tempts them with apple tarts, meringues, chocolate mousse, Black Forest cake, rice pudding, creamy Swiss rolls and mountains of profiteroles.

In Donizetti's L'elisir d'amore (Elixir of Love) the townspeople don't wait for Adina's wedding to indulge. At the opening of Act II, they lavish in an extravagant prenuptial feast as Adina and Belcore are about to sign the marriage contract. The traveling salesman, Dulcamara and purveyor of the titular love elixir sings, "Weddings are all very nice. But what I like best about them is the pleasant sight of the banquet."

One of the most significant meals in both opera and American diplomacy comes at the end of Act I of John Adams's *Nixon in China*. "The world watches and listens, we must seize the hour," sings Nixon as he toasts his host Prime Minister Chou En-Lai before the banquet. The act ends as the government officials sit down to a feast of spongy bamboo shoots, shark fin soup, roast pork and Chinese sausage.

The official menu from The Nixon Foundation was spongy bamboo shoots and egg-white consommé, shark's fin in three shreds, fried and stewed prawns, mushrooms and mustard green, steamed chicken with coconut, almond junket, pastries, fruits.

Opera companies have to put these meals on stage as they are part of the production and often provide real food. The Metropolitan Opera in New York City has a fully functional backstage kitchen for meeting the culinary demands of librettos. For the singers, eating onstage has its perils and singers regularly face the challenge of timing bites between musical phrases. Timing is the key, singers need to determine what they can eat and swallow between lines. Some singers prefer to eat as the libretto calls for ensuring a truly authentic performance. Many singers generally eat lightly before a performance and during a three hour opera performance, stage food comes in handy.

Many singers have requests, especially for wine stand-ins. Favorites are flat soda (to prevent burping while singing), iced tea and apple juice. The bass-baritone Luca Pisaroni, playing Leporello in *Don Giovanni*, asked for vegetable sausage and bass-baritone James Morris prefers bananas while playing Scarpia in the fatal meal scene of Puccini's *Tosca*.

The singers in *Hansel & Gretel* try to avoid swallowing a lot of the pastry due to dairy products creating phlegm which can make it difficult to sing. A trick when drinking milk, breathe out through the nose to avoid inhaling it. One singer even developed a technique to appear to be eating on stage but smeared a lot of it all over her face. The tricks of the trade.

Conceived by Sylvia Volk, a lifelong opera devotee, with Wayne Line and Eileen Breen compiling and editing.

Listen and Enjoy.

Operas to Dine With

Aida

by Giuseppe Verdi
p. 33

Appetizer
Yogurt Cucumber Dip

Entrée
Kofta

Side Dish
Root Vegetable Salad
Fattoush

Dessert
Umm Ali

Billy Budd

by Benjamin Britten
p. 39

Appetizer
Seamen's Platter
Ships Biscuits

Entrée
Corned Beef & Cabbage

Dessert
Bread & Butter Pudding

Carmen

by Georges Bizet
p. 43

Cocktail Appetizer
Carmen's Sangria

Entrée
Paella

Dessert
Leche Frita

Das Rheingold

by Richard Wagner
p. 49

Cocktail Appetizer
Soma

Entrée
Anise Pork with Figs & Golden Apples

Dessert
Ambrosia

Don Giovanni
by Wolfgang Amadeus Mozart
p. 53

Appetizer
Antipasto

Entrée
Italian Roast Duck

Side Dish
Roast Vegetable
French Turnips

Dessert
Zuppa Inglese

Eugene Onegin
by Pyotr Il'yich Tchaikovsky
p. 61

Appetizer
Mushroom Caviar

Entrée
Beef Stroganoff

Dessert
Sharlotka

Falstaff

by Giuseppe Verdi
p. 67

Appetizer
Sir John's Salad

Entrée
Falstaff's Fig & Prosciutto Penne

Dessert
Aniseed Cake

Halka

by Stanislaw Moniuszko
p. 71

Appetizer
Bigos

Entrée
Potato Cheese Pierogi

Dessert
Apple Strudel

Il Trovatore
by Giuseppe Verdi
p. 79

Appetizer
Gypsy Soup

Entrée
Chicken Mushroom Cobbler with Gruyere Herb Biscuits

Dessert
Strawberry Gypsy Pie

La Boheme
by Giacomo Puccini
p. 87

Appetizer
Cheese Fondue

Entrée
Chicken Morengo

Dessert
Profiteroles

La Traviata
by Giacomo Puccini
p. 91

Appetizer
Minestrone alla Trovatore

Entrée
Boneless Pork with Vegetables

Dessert
Poached Pears in Spiced Brown Sugar Syrup

Madame Butterfly
by Giacomo Puccini
p. 97

Appetizer
Miso Soup

Entrée
Roasted Orange Chicken

Dessert
Fruit Sando

Marriage of Figaro
by Wolfgang Amadeus Mozart
p. 103

Appetizer
Italian Wedding Soup

Entrée
Prime Rib Roast

Side Dish
Mashed Potatoes
Buttered Baby Carrots

Dessert
Cheese & Fruit Plate

Susannah
by Carlisle Floyd
p. 109

Appetizer
Mustard Greens
Cornbread

Entrée
Southern Fried Chicken

Side Dish
Succotash

Dessert
Skillet Peaches

Tosca

by Giacomo Puccini
p. 115

Appetizer
Arugula with Brûléed Figs, Ricotta, Prosciutto
& Smoked Marzipan

Entrée
Baked Whole Fish with Truffles

Dessert
Tosca Cake

Historical Opera Dishes from the Artists

by Sylvia Volk

p. 123

Casanova's Suckling Veal Liver

Giacomo Casanova, Italian Librettist

Naples Style Bucatini

Enrique Caruso, Tenor

Risotto Verdi Style
Spalla Cotta

Giuseppe Verdi, Italian Composer

Rossini's Tournedos

Gioacchino Rossini, Italian Composer

Spaghetti alla Gennaro

Antonio De Curtis (Totò), Italian Opera Singer

Tuscan Cibreo

Catherine De'Medici, Italian Patron of the Arts

Opera Singers Favourites

p. 137

Alfredo Sauce & Fettuccini

Wayne Line, Baritone

Classic Bread Pudding with Vanilla Sauce

Jacqueline Ornsby, Soprano

Friûlan Polenta

Suzanne Fatta, Bass

Pasta e Fagioli

Salvatore Licitra, Tenor

Puccini Primavera

Valerian Ruminski, Bass

Rueben Slaw

Jacqueline Quirk, Soprano

Opera Buffs Obsessions
p. 145

Cream of Chicken Broccoli Soup
Hedy Kuntsman, Friend of Delaware Opera

Del Posto's Fusili with Pesto & Peperonata
Sylvia Volk

La Pizza Con Funghi
Seymour Barab

Lasagna
Margaret Breen, Nickel City Opera Volunteer, Soprano

Sopa de Elote
Rose Betty Williams, Austin Opera Guild
Opera Volunteers International

Spinach, Beet & Quinoa Salad
Colleen Eder, Dietician Consultant,
Erie County Senior Services

Wild Mushroom Pizza with Carmelized Onion, Fontina & Rosemary Pizza
Seymour Barab

Opera Sweets

by Sylvia Volk

p. 157

Fudge

Chocolate Opera Fudge

Vanilla Opera Fudge

Opera BonBons

Opera Creams

After the Opera Favorites

p. 163

Almond Chocolate Chip Opera Cookies

Danielle DiStefano, Soprano

Blueberry Streusel Pie

Hedy Kunstman, friend of Delaware Valley Opera

Chocolate Gâteau

Evelyn Franz

Lemon Curd Opera Cake with Chocolate Buttercream

Sylvia Volk

Opera Blondies

Ruth Newman

Opera Cake

Danielle DiStefano, Soprano

Peach Melba

Sylvia Volk

Sarah Bernhardt Cookies

Sylvia Volk

Almond Thumbprint Opera Cookies

Marie Rose, Austin Opera Guild

The Opera Cocktail

from Sylvia Volk

p. 181

Bellini Cocktail

Fresh Peach & Raspberry Bellini

Strawberry Bellini

Bellini Schnapps

Operas To Dine With

Aida

by Giuseppe Verdi

Opera in four acts. Libretto by Antonio Ghislanzoni, outline by Auguste Mariette (Mariette Bey), with development of the material by the composer and by Camille Du Locle. First performance at the Cairo Opera House on 24th December 1871.

In the Egypt of the Pharoahs there is war with Ethiopia. The Ethiopian King's daughter Aida, has been captured and is now a slave in the service of the Pharoah's daughter, Amneris. Radames loves Aida but is loved by Amneris. He is appointed general of the Egyptian army and in the second scene of the second act returns in triumph, to be rewarded by the unwelcome hand of Amneris in marriage. Aida's father Amonasro has been taken prisoner, his life spared at the intercession of Radames.

In the third act he induces his daughter to help him discover the plans of the Egyptian army which she does in a meeting with Radames, their conversation overheard by Amonasro. Aida and Amonasro take flight but the apparent treachery of Radames is now revealed and he is condemned to death to the dismay of Amneris. In the final scene he is immured in a stone tomb where he is joined by Aida. As they die, Amneris, above the tomb, prays for peace for her beloved Radames.

Verdi wrote his Egyptian opera Aida in response to a commission from the Khedive of Egypt for the opening of the new Cairo Opera House after rejecting requests for an anthem to celebrate the opening of the Suez Canal a year earlier.
The first performance was conducted by the famous double-bass player Bottesini.

Spectacle of which some stage directors have made much is provided particularly in the return of the victorious Radames in triumph. The story was the invention of the French Egyptologist Auguste Mariette elaborated in French prose by Camille Du Locle before the final Italian text was drafted.

Aida remains a popular part of Italian opera repertoire. Familiar concert excerpts from Aida inevitably include the tenor Celeste Aida (Heavenly Aida) and Aida's Ritorna vincitor (Return victorious). The grand march has celebrated many an non-operatic festivity and has allowed spectacular extravagance in more ostentatious productions of the opera. O patria mia (O my homeland) for Aida in the third act adds a particular poignancy while the final death scene of Radames and Aida is also sometimes to be heard in dramatic isolation.

Appetizer
Yogurt Cucumber Dip

Ingredients
- 2 cups yogurt
- 1 large cucumber, seeded, grated
- 10 large mint leaves, minced
- 1 clove garlic, crushed
- ½ teaspoon salt

Directions
- Mix all ingredients together, chill for 1-2 hours.

Helpful Hints
For thicker dip: put yogurt into cheese cloth, drain several hours.
Place cucumber in tea towel, wring out excess moisture.

Serve
With pita bread cut into triangles.

Entrée
Kofta

Ingredients

- 1 pound ground beef
- ¼ pound ground lamb, optional if not using add more ground beef
- ½ cup parsley, minced
- 1 small onion, grated
- 2 garlic cloves, minced
- ½ teaspoon cumin powder
- 1 teaspoon nutmeg
- 1 tablespoon salt
- 1 teaspoon crushed black pepper

Directions

- Mix onions, garlic, spices together, let rest a few minutes. Add meat, parsley to onion mixture, mix well. Shape meat into kofta shapes , 2-3 inch, cigar shape.
- Coat bottom of large pan with olive oil, heat over medium high heat. Add koftas to pan, fry on all sides. Cover pan, cook additional 5 mins.
- Uncover pan, cook until liquid evaporates.

Side Dish
Root Vegetables Salad

Ingredients

- 3 small beets
- 3 small potatoes
- 3 medium carrots
- ¼ cup olive oil
- 2 garlic cloves, crushed
- ¼ cup cilantro or parsley, chopped
- ½ lime, cut in two wedges
- Salt, pepper & cumin to taste

Directions
- Peel vegetables, place in saucepan, cover with water.
- Bring to boil over high heat. Lower heat, cook until knife inserts easily into vegetables. Drain, cut into bite size pieces.
- In large bowl, mix garlic, salt, pepper, cumin. Squeeze lime into mixture, whisk together. Add olive oil, whisk until combined, season to taste. Pour mixture over vegetables, toss.

Side Dish
Fattoush

Ingredients
- 2 loaves pita bread
- Extra virgin olive oil
- ½ teaspoon sumac
- 1 heart romaine lettuce, chopped
- 1 english cucumber, cut in small cubes
- 6 roma tomatoes, cut in small cubes
- 5 green onions, chopped
- 5 radishes, stems removed, sliced thin
- 2 cups parsley, chopped
- 1 cup mint leaves, chopped
- Salt & pepper

Dressing
- 1½ limes, juiced
- ¼ cup extra virgin olive oil
- 1 teaspoon sumac
- ¼ teaspoon cinnamon
- Salt & pepper

Directions
- In large skillet, heat 3 tablespoons olive oil. Break pia into bite size pieces, fry until browned, tossing frequently.

- Add salt & pepper, ½ teaspoon of sumac. Remove pita chips, drain on paper towel.
- In large salad bowl mix lettuce, cucumber, tomatoes, green onions, radishes, parsley, toss lightly.

Dressing
- Whisk all ingredients together. Pour over salad, toss lightly. Add pita chips, toss again. Serve.

Dessert

Umm Ali

Ingredients
- 1 (17.25 ounce) package frozen puff pastry, thawed
- 5 cups milk
- 1 cup white sugar
- 1 teaspoon vanilla extract
- ¼ cup raisins
- ¼ cup slivered almonds
- ¼ cup pine nuts
- ¼ cup chopped pistachio nuts
- ¼ cup sweetened, flaked coconut

Directions
- Preheat oven to 400°F. Unroll puff pastry sheets, place on baking sheet. Bake for 15 mins until golden brown, let cool slightly. Break into pieces, place in large mixing bowl.
- Add raisins, almonds, pine nuts, pistachios, coconut, toss lightly. Pour into 9x13 inch glass baking pan, spread evenly.
- In saucepan, add milk, sugar, vanilla. Heat to steaming, not boiled. Pour over mixture in baking pan, bake 15 minutes.
- Turn oven to broil until top is brown, 2-3 minutes. Remove from oven, let rest for 5-10 minutes.

Billy Budd
by Benjamin Britten

Benjamin Britten. Opera in four acts 1951. Revised version in two acts 1960. Libretto by E.M. Forster & Eric Crozier after Herman Melville's story of the same title. First performance at the Royal Opera House, Covent Garden, London, 1st December 1951. First performance of the revised version, 9th January 1964.

Set on HMS Indomitable in 1797 during the French wars, the drama involves the relationship between Edward Fairfax Vere and the seaman Billy Budd, a sailor who has been taken to serve in the navy. Billy Budd, a character of radiant innocence, is in conflict with Claggart, the evil master-at-arms who resolves to destroy him. Struck by Billy Budd, Claggart is killed and Captain Vere, who is aware of Billy Budd's innate goodness and innocence, is compelled by duty to sentence him to death.

The opera, set on a warship, has only men in the cast. It deals, as so often in Britten's operas, with the destruction of innocence. Both that of the Novice, forced through fear to betray Billy Budd and that of Billy Budd himself. Captain Vere is presented with what might be seen as the traditional conflict between duty and love, current in earlier operatic tradition.

The technical problem of writing only for male voices is triumphantly overcome while the work provided a moving role for Peter Pears as Captain Vere in the original production and a chance for Britten again to evoke the sea as he had done in Peter Grimes six years before.

Appetizer
Seaman's Platter

Ingredients

- 1 onion, sliced in rings
- 2 tablespoons white wine vinegar
- 4 eggs, hard cooked, peeled, cut in half
- 8 ounces sliced ham or other meats
- 4 ounces sliced English cheese; Cheddar, Stilton or Wensleydale
- 4-8 pieces seasonal fruit
- 4-8 baby pickled cucumbers
- ½ cup English pickle
- 4 tablespoons butter, cut in pats
- Salt & pepper

Instructions

- In small bowl, place onion slices, pour over vinegar. Season to taste with salt & pepper. Marinade 30 mins.
- On four platters, boards or dinner plates, divide eggs, ham, cheese, bread, fruit, pickled cucumber. Divide English pickle into four small dishes or ramekins. Place ramekin, pat of butter on each plate. Divide pickled onions among four plates, serve immediately.

Helpful Hint

Marinating onions in vinegar removes some of the bitterness and heat.

Serve

With Ship's Biscuits.

Ship's Biscuits

Ingredients

- 2 cups flour
- ½ teaspoon salt
- ½ to ¾ cups water

Directions

- Preheat oven to 250°F.
- Mix flour, salt together. Add enough water to make a very stiff dough. Knead a few minutes, use rolling pin until flat, ½ inch thick, cut into 2 inch x 2 inch sections.
- Punch full of holes with fork.
- Bake in ungreased, flat pan 2-3 hours.

Entree
Corned Beef & Cabbage

Ingredients

- 4 pounds corned beef brisket
- 3 onions
- 1 onion, stuck with cloves
- 6 carrots
- 6 potatoes, medium
- 2 pounds cabbage
- 1 teaspoon thyme
- Butter, to taste
- Salt & pepper, to taste

Directions

- Fill large pot with cold water, add beef, spices. Bring to boil.
- Add onions, carrots, return to boil, simmer, three hours.
- Remove cloved onion. Quarter cabbage, potatoes, add to pot, simmer ½ hour until cabbage, potatoes are tender. Drain.

Serve

Dot with butter, salt & pepper.

Dessert
Bread & Butter Pudding
Ingredients
- 10 slices of bread
- 1¼ cups milk
- ¼ cup butter, melted
- ½ cup brown sugar
- 1 egg, beaten
- 2 teaspoons mixed spice
- 1 cup mixed dried fruit
- 2 teaspoons mixed spice
- 1½ teaspoon orange zest, grated
- ½ teaspoon nutmeg

Directions
- Preheat oven to 350°F. Butter 1½ quart baking dish.
- Cut crusts from bread, tear bread into pieces, place in medium size bowl, cover with milk. Let rest 30 minutes.
- In another medium bowl, beat melted butter, sugar, mixed spice, egg together until smooth.
- Toss with soaked bread and milk. Stir in dried fruit, orange zest.
- Pour into prepared dish, sprinkle with nutmeg.
- Bake 75 minutes, until set.

Carmen

by Georges Bizet

Opéra comique in four acts. 1874.
Libretto by Henri Meilhac & Ludovic Halévy, after the novel by
Prosper Mérimée. First performance by the Opéra-Comique at
the Salle Favart, Paris, on 3rd March 1875.

Set in Seville around the year 1830, the opera deals with the love and jealousy of Don José, who is lured away from his duty as a soldier and his beloved Micaëla by the gypsy factory girl Carmen, whom he allows to escape from custody. He is later induced to join the smugglers with whom Carmen is associated but is driven wild by jealousy. This comes to a head when Carmen makes clear her preference for the bull-fighter Escamillo. The last act outside the bull-ring in Seville brings Escamillo to the arena accompanied by Carmen, there stabbed to death by Don José who has been awaiting her arrival.

Carmen, the most famous of Bizet's operas, with its exotic Spanish setting, introduced a note of realism into opera that proved unacceptable to many who saw the first performances. Objection was taken to the wild and immoral behavior of Carmen, the chorus of cigarette-factory girls, their smoking and the final murder of Carmen on the stage.

Orchestral suites have been derived from the score, while popular excerpts must include Carmen's seductive Habanera and Seguidilla the famous Toreador's Song and Don José's later reference to the flower Carmen had once thrown him, La fleur que tu m'avais jetée (The flower that you threw me), with Micaëla's moving aria Je dis que rien ne m'épouvante (I say that nothing frightens me).

Carmen's Sangria

Ingredients

- One 750-ml bottle red wine
- ¾ cup brandy or cognac
- ¼ cup orange liqueur such as Cointreau
- ¼ cup orange juice, freshly squeezed
- ¼ cup pomegranate juice
- 1 cup lemon soda
- 1 peach, sliced
- 1 orange, thinly sliced
- 1 lemon, thinly sliced
- 1 lime, thinly sliced

Directions

- In glass pitcher, combine wine, brandy, liqueur, juices. Add lemon soda, fruit. Stir in frozen juice cubes or ice.

Helpful Hints

Make ahead of time, chill.

Instead of adding ice, watering down sangria, make frozen juice cubes with pomegranate juice.

Entree
Paella

Ingredients

- 1 cup fresh parsley, chopped
- ¼ cup fresh lemon juice
- 3 garlic cloves, minced
- 1 cup water
- 1 teaspoon saffron threads
- 48 ounces chicken broth
- ½ pound jumbo shrimp
- 4 chicken thighs, skinned, boned, cut in half
- 2 links Spanish chorizo, cut into ½ inch thick slices (for less spicy use 6" of Kielbasa)

- 1 6 ounce prosciutto, cut into 1 inch cubes
- 2 cups onion, finely chopped
- 1 cup red bell pepper, finely chopped
- 1 8 ounce can tomatoes, diced with liquid
- 4 garlic cloves, minced
- 3 cups Arborio rice, uncooked
- 1 cup frozen peas
- 8-10 mussels scrubbed, debearded
- ¼ cup fresh lemon juice
- Olive oil

Directions

- In small bowl, combine first four ingredients set aside.
- In large saucepan, combine water, saffron, broth, bring to simmer, not to boil, keep warm over low heat.
- Peel, devein shrimp, leave tails intact, set aside.
- In large skillet heat 1 tablespoon oil over medium heat.
- Add chicken, saute 3 minutes each side, remove chicken from pan, set aside. Add sausage, prosciutto to pan, saute 2 minutes, remove from pan, set aside.
- Reduce heat to medium low, add onion, bell pepper, saute 15 minutes stirring occasionally. Add garlic, continue to saute 1 minute. Add tomatoes, cook 5 minutes. Add rice, cook 2 minutes stirring constantly.
- Stir in herb blend from first step with broth mixture, chicken, sausage, peas. Bring to boil, cook 10-15 minutes.
- Arrange mussels in pan, pushing them slightly into rice mixture. Cook until shells open, about 5-6 minutes. If any of the shells do not open take them out, dispose.
- Add shrimp, cook 5-6 minutes until pink, indicating they are cooked. Remove from heat, pour lemon juice over mixture.

- Cover, let stand 10-15 minutes allowing any moisture to absorb.

Serve

With warm, crusty bread.

Dessert
Leche Frita
Fried Milk

Ingredients
- 3½ tablespoons cornstarch
- 7 tablespoons all-purpose flour, divided
- ½ cup sugar
- 1 quart whole milk, divided
- 1 cinnamon stick
- 2 large eggs, room temperature
- ¼ cup olive oil, for frying
- 2 tablespoons butter
- Ground cinnamon for garnish

Directions
- In a large bowl, whisk together cornstarch, 3½ tablespoons flour, sugar. Add 1 cup milk, mix well with whisk, let stand until thickened approximately 10 minutes.
- In large saucepan, heat rest of milk, cinnamon stick over medium-low heat. When milk begins to bubble, remove from heat, strain little by little into sugar/flour mixture, stirring constantly.
- Pour sugar/flour/milk mixture back into saucepan over low heat, stirring well for 10 minutes.
- Lightly oil 9x9 glass baking dish with olive oil, pour in leche frita mixture to a depth of ¾ inch. Leave to cool in refrigerator for at least 3 hours or overnight.
- Run knife around edge of leche frita to ensure it's not

sticking, very quickly turning it out on counter. Cut into 2¼ inches squares. In a 9-inch pan, this should create a 16 piece 4 by 4 grid.

- In medium size bowl, beat eggs.
- Heat olive oil in frying pan to a depth approaching ¼ inch over medium heat, add butter.
- In separate bowl add remaining flour. Dip in beaten eggs then bread each square in remaining flour. Fry in hot oil for 1 minute on each side until lightly golden.
- Sprinkle with ground cinnamon, serve immediately or allow to cool, serve at room temperature.

Das Rheingold
by Richard Wagner

*Vorabend (Prologue) to Der Ring des Nibelungen
(The Ring of the Nibelung) in four scenes.1854.
Libretto by the composer. First performance at the Königliches
Hofund Nationaltheater, Munich, on 22nd September 1869.*

The Rhinemaidens, guardians of the Rhinegold, swim in the waters teasing the Nibelung Alberich. Revealing the secret of the gold that he who forges a ring from it will rule the world but the one who forges the ring must abjure love. Alberich seizes the gold and makes off. Wotan and Fricka awake from their sleep and see the new castle completed. Its builders Fasolt and Fafner must be rewarded with Fricka's sister Freia, who seeks escape from the bargain. Her brothers Donner and Froh try to protect her but the two giants insist on their reward. Fasolt hoping thus to deprive the gods of youth, imparted by the apples that Freia has in her possession.

Loge had hoped to find fault with the castle in order to secure Freia's release. He tells the other gods of Alberich's forging of the ring and renunciation of love which will bring him power over the world and suggests that it can easily be stolen from the Nibelung. The giants decide that they would accept the ring instead of Freia but take her away with them as a hostage until this can be accomplished. Wotan decides that he will go with Loge to the home of the Nibelung.

There is hammering in the realm of Alberich where Mime has been made to forge a gold net, the Tarncap, which Alberich dons thereby making himself invisible.

Wotan and Loge arrive and learn from Mime of Alberich's cruel tyranny over the Nibelung. When Alberich returns Loge tricks him into transforming himself into a toad, which they then seize, snatching the Tarncap from his head and restoring him as a captive to his original shape. In the realm of the gods Alberich is forced to surrender the ring on which he puts a curse. With Alberich's gold and eventually with the ring itself Wotan buys back Freia's freedom. Fafner quarrels with his brother over the division of the spoil and kills him. Wotan names his new castle Valhalla and leads the others into it while Loge contemplates return to his original form, as fire, to consume Valhalla as fate has decreed.

The first of the four dramas of Wagner's tetralogy sets the scene for what is to follow. The music brings together a series of motifs that will reappear in the later parts of the cycle. In a work that follows the principles laid down in his own writings, rules to which he does not elsewhere strictly adhere in view of the musical difficulties they present. Excerpts from the opera that may be heard in concert recital include Erda's warning to Wotan, Weiche, Wotan, weiche! (Yield it, Wotan, yield it!) as she urges him to give up the ring and the treasure he has taken from Alberich, Wotan's greeting to Valhalla, Abendlich strahlt der Sonne Auge (At evening the eye of the sun shines) and the entrance of the gods into Valhalla, this last often in an orchestral version.

Appetizer Cocktail
Soma

Ingredients
- 2 cups whole milk, preferably raw or non-homogenized
- 3 whole dates, pitted
- ¼ cup almonds
- ½ teaspoon ground turmeric

- 2-3 tablespoons organic rose water
- 3 cardamom, whole pods
- 1-2 ounce bourbon

Directions

- In blender, combine dates, almonds.
- In medium saucepan, bring milk, herbs to gentle boil, remove from heat. Add date/almond mixture, bourbon to milk mixture, blend until smooth and frothy.

Serve

In goblets.

Entree
Anise Pork with Figs & Golden Apples

Ingredients

- 4 6 ounce boneless pork loin steaks
- 1 cup golden apple slices, ¼ inch thick
- 4 dried Calimyrna figs, quartered
- ¾ teaspoon aniseed or fennel seeds, crushed
- 1 tablespoon olive oil
- 2 tablespoons unsalted butter
- 2 large shallots, thinly sliced
- 1 large garlic clove, minced
- ½ cup fresh orange juice
- 1 tablespoon red wine vinegar
- Salt & pepper

Directions

- Sprinkle aniseed on both sides of pork chops, season with salt & pepper.
- In large skillet, heat olive oil until almost smoking. Add pork steaks, cook over moderately high heat, turning once, until well browned about 3 minutes per side. Reduce heat to moderate, cook until firm, barely pink inside, about 4 minutes longer. Transfer to a plate.
- Melt 1 tablespoon butter in skillet, add shallots, cook

over moderate heat until softened, about 4 minutes. Add garlic, cook until fragrant, about 1 minute. Add apple slices, cook, turning, until lightly browned, about 2 minutes. Add 2 tablespoons of orange juice, cook until apple slices are just tender, about 1 minute. Add figs, remaining 6 tablespoons orange juice, increase heat to moderately high, simmer to blend flavors, 1 to 2 minutes.

- Season with vinegar, salt & pepper. Swirl in remaining 1 tablespoon butter. Return pork, juices to skillet, reheat briefly before serving.

Serve

With white or wild rice.

Dessert
Ambrosia

Ingredients
- 1 can pineapple, tidbits or cubed, drained
- 1 can mandarin orange slices
- 1 cup coconut, shredded
- 1 cup mini marshmallows
- 1 8 ounce container sour cream

Directions
- Mix all ingredients in large bowl, cover, refrigerate at least 2 hours prior to serving.

Helpful Hint

Try plain yogurt instead of sour cream.

Don Giovanni

by Wolfgang Amadeus Mozart

Dramma giocoso (opera buffa) in two acts. Libretto by Lorenzo Da Ponte. First performance at the Estates Theatre, Prague, on 29th October 1787.

Don Giovanni has had his way with Donna Anna entering her bedroom when she mistook him for her betrothed, Don Ottavio. Leporello, outside, complains of his life as a servant. Donna Anna pursues Don Giovanni and is joined by her father who dies as they fight. Don Ottavio joins her in vowing revenge against the unknown assailant while Don Giovanni and Leporello make their escape. Now they come across another woman, Donna Elvira, an earlier victim of Don Giovanni who runs off when they recognize each other while Leporello reads her a catalogue of his master's conquests.

Master and servant next come across a group of peasants ready to celebrate the marriage of Zerlina and Masetto. Don Giovanni manages to be left alone with Zerlina, having invited the whole company to his palace nearby. As they go off together Donna Elvira appears intervening to warn the girl. Donna Anna and Don Ottavio join them, recognizing Don Giovanni by his voice.

In Don Giovanni's garden, Masetto reproaches Zerlina frustrating Don Giovanni's attempts to lure her away. Donna Anna, Donna Elvira and Don Ottavio appear, masked and are invited by Leporello to join the celebration. At the ball in the palace Don Giovanni takes Zerlina into another room and when she screams pretends that Leporello is guilty. The three masked visitors reveal themselves and accuse Don Giovanni.

Outside Donna Elvira's house, Leporello is made to impersonate his master to woo her while Don Giovanni turns his attention to her maid, a cruel deception. Masetto, seeking Don Giovanni, has his helpers sent off in various directions by Don Giovanni in the guise of Leporello. When Masetto is alone he sets upon him, leaving him to be consoled by Zerlina. Leporello, taking refuge in the courtyard of the house of Donna Anna is seized but pleads for mercy when they realize who he is.

As night draws on, Don Giovanni and Leporello now come together in a churchyard where the stone statue on the tomb of the Commendatore is heard to speak. At this Don Giovanni tells Leporello to invite the statue to dinner. The statue accepts and in a final scene is heard slowly approaching the room where Don Giovanni is at dinner to the terror first of Donna Elvira, who has been urging reform on her betrayal and then of Leporello. The statue slowly enters and holding Don Giovanni's hand takes him into the fiery pit that now opens before them. There follows a brief epilogue in which the moral of the tale is pointed by those who remain.

Il dissoluto punito, ossia Il Don Giovanni (The Libertine Punished, or Don Giovanni) was written for Prague and staged in Vienna the following year with additional arias for Don Ottavio and Donna Elvira. Lorenzo Da Ponte based his libretto on the well-known story, dramatized in the 17th century by the Spanish playwright Tirso da Molina and the subject of an opera by Giuseppe Gazzaniga with a libretto by Giovanni Bertati performed in Venice, February 1787.

Da Ponte also drew on Molière's treatment of the subject. The opera opens with a sinister overture in which the approach of the stone statue can be heard.

Don Ottavio's two great arias, Dalla sua pace (Of her peace) written for Vienna and Il mio tesoro (My treasure) are essential parts of tenor repertoire.

The buffo Leporello's catalogue song, Madamina il catalogo (Miss, the catalogue) provides bass-baritones with superb opportunity for comedy. Don Giovanni's Là ci darem la mano (You'll give me your hand, my dear) the subject, among other things, of variations by Beethoven and by Chopin and elaboration by Liszt is one of the most famous of all operatic songs. Don Giovanni orders celebration in an energetic Finch'han dal vino (Let them have wine) and woos Donna Elvira's maid in an eloquent serenade, Deh, vieni alla finestra (Come to the window). Donna Anna herself has her moment in Or sai chi l'onore (You know for sure) while Zerlina's Batti, batti, o bel Masetto (Beat me, beat me, fair Masetto) teases the poor man into easy submission.

Appetizer
Antipasto

Ingredients
- Italian meats, prosciutto, salami, capocollo, sliced
- Pickled vegetables
- Black olives
- Green olives
- Cheese, sliced
- Italian bread
- Assorted crackers

Directions
- Place several slices of meat, pickled vegetables, olives, cheese on individual plates.

Serve
With sliced Italian bread, crackers.

Entree
Italian Roast Duck

Ingredients
- 1 Duckling or Duck, about 4 pounds
- 4-5 oranges, juiced
- ⅓ cup cognac
- 1 6 inch sprig fresh rosemary, cut in ½ inches
- ¼ cup butter, melted
- 2 small carrots, to absorb grease
- Salt & fresh ground black pepper

Directions
- Preheat oven 350°F. Line roasting pan with foil.
- Rub duck inside and out with salt & pepper, place rosemary in cavity.
- In small bowl combine orange juice, melted butter, cognac for basting.
- Place duck, carrots in roasting pan. Roast for 2 hours basting every 20 minutes with orange mixture.
- When done, remove from oven, let sit 10 minutes prior to carving.

Side Dish
Roast Vegetables

Ingredients
- 3 potatoes, cut in bite size pieces
- 3 carrots, cut in bite size pieces,
- 1 large Spanish onion, cut in chunks
- 2 cloves garlic, crushed
- 2 tablespoons butter
- Olive oil
- Salt & pepper

Directions
- Preheat oven to 350°F. Line baking sheet with parchment paper.

- In large bowl, add potatoes, carrots, onions, crushed garlic, olive oil, toss gently.
- Pour all onto parchment paper, add dabs of butter on top. Roast for 1 hour.

Helpful Hint

When in oven, start French Turnip below.

French Turnip

Ingredients
- Turnip, medium size, peel, cut in small pieces
- 1 tablespoon apple cider vinegar
- 2 tablespoons butter
- 2 tablespoons flour
- 2 cups milk
- 2 cups mozzarella cheese, shredded
- Salt & pepper

Directions
- In medium saucepan, boil turnip in water for 20 minutes until soft. Drain, mash.
- Place in oven proof dish add apple cider vinegar, stir.
- In medium saucepan, melt butter over medium heat, add flour. Cook for 3 minutes, stirring constantly. Slowly add milk, stirring constantly until all added. Add salt & pepper to taste.
- Pour over turnip, spread cheese on top of mixture.
- Bake at 350°F for ½ hour. Broil top for 5 minutes to brown cheese.

Dessert
Zuppa Inglese

Ingredients
- 1 9 inch sponge cake, approximately 3 inches high

For pastry creams:
- 4 cups milk, full fat

- 1 cup & 6 tablespoons sugar
- 10 large egg yolks
- ⅔ cup all purpose flour
- 3 ounces semisweet chocolate, chopped
- ½ teaspoon ground cinnamon
- 2 teaspoons vanilla extract
- 1 teaspoon orange peel, grated

For syrup:
- 1 cup & 2 tablespoons water
- ¾ cup sugar
- ½ cup dark rum

For serving:
- 2 cups whipping cream, chilled
- Chocolate shavings, optional
- Chopped candied fruit, optional

Directions

For pastry creams:
- In large, heavy saucepan bring milk, ½ cup plus 3 tablespoons sugar to boil, stirring to dissolve sugar, remove from heat.
- In large bowl, whisk yolks with remaining ½ cup plus 3 tablespoons sugar to blend. Sift flour into yolk mixture, whisk to blend. Gradually whisk in hot milk mixture.
- Return mixture to saucepan, whisk over medium heat until custard boils, thickens, about 2 minutes.
- In 2 medium bowls, divide custard. To one bowl, add chocolate, cinnamon, stir until chocolate melts. To second bowl, add vanilla, orange peel, stir to blend. Press plastic wrap onto surface of each custard, chill until cold, at least 4 hours.

For syrup:
- In heavy medium saucepan, stir water, sugar over medium heat until sugar dissolves. Increase heat, bring

to boil, cool. Mix in rum.

To assemble:

- Cut sponge cake vertically in ⅜ inch thick slices. In 16 cup glass bowl, arrange enough cake slices on bottom to cover in single layer, brush 6 tablespoons syrup over cake slices, spread half of orange cream over cake.
- Top with another layer of cake slices, brush with 7 tablespoons syrup, spread remaining chocolate cream over.
- Top with another layer of cake slices, brush with 7 tablespoons syrup, spread remaining orange cream over.
- Top with another layer of cake slices, brush with 7 tablespoons syrup, spread remaining chocolate cream over.
- Top with enough remaining cake slices to cover. Brush 7 tablespoons syrup over. Cover, refrigerate at least 2 hours or overnight.

Serve

In medium bowl, whip 2 cups chilled cream to soft peaks. Spread cream over cake, garnish with chocolate shavings and candied fruit.

Eugene Onegin

by Pyotr Il'yich Tchaikovsky

Opera in three acts. 1878. Libretto by the composer and Konstantin Stepanovich Shilovsky, after Pushkin's verse novel. First performance at the Bol'shoy Theatre, Moscow, on 23rd January 1881.

At Madame Larina's country house, Onegin and Lensky arrive. Lensky to join his betrothed Olga, leaving Onegin to talk to Tatyana who falls in love as her old nurse Filipyevna realizes. In her bedroom she writes a letter to Onegin which Filipyevna is to deliver. In the garden she meets him and he discourages her urging patient restraint and telling her he has no mind to marry.

At a ball in the house to celebrate Tatyana's birthday, Onegin chooses to dance with Olga to Lensky's increasing anger leading to his demand for satisfaction. The next morning the two men fight a duel and Lensky is killed.

The third act takes place some years later at a more fashionable ball in St Petersburg. Onegin is there having returned from self-imposed exile. The ball is also attended by his kinsman Prince Gremin and his wife Tatyana, her presence arousing Onegin's love. He writes her a letter declaring his passion but she reminds him of his former advice to her and whatever her real feelings, now rejects him.

Tchaikovsky's opera was written at the difficult period of his marriage to an apparently infatuated and certainly unbalanced admirer and their immediate separation. It was completed abroad in Switzerland and Italy. Onegin's subsequent answer in the garden.

Prince Gremin's aria in the third act gives depth to his character as he describes the effect on him of his marriage to the young Tatyana. The dances from the two ball scenes have provided concert audiences with orchestral excerpts from the score.

Appetizer
Mushroom Caviar with Blini

Ingredients
- 4½ ounce mushrooms, dried
- 1 large onion, finely chopped
- 4 tablespoons sunflower oil
- 2 large garlic gloves, chopped
- 2 tablespoons vinegar
- Salt & pepper

Directions
- Wash mushrooms, add to shallow bowl with cold water to just cover, let soak for 2-3 hours.
- Drain water off into medium saucepan. Rinse mushrooms, finely chop, add to saucepan. Boil, simmer until water evaporates, mushrooms are tender. Remove from heat, cool.
- In medium saute pan, saute onions until translucent.
- In medium bowl, add mushrooms, onions, garlic, vinegar, sunflower oil, salt & pepper mixing well. Chill well.

Blini

Ingredients
- 1 cup all-purpose flour
- ¾ teaspoon salt
- ½ teaspoon baking powder
- ¾ cup milk
- 2 tablespoons milk
- 1 large egg

- 1 tablespoon unsalted butter, melted
- 1 tablespoon unsalted butter
- Sour cream, for serving

Directions

- In large bowl, combine flour, salt, baking powder.
- In separate large bowl, whisk ¾ cup plus 2 tablespoons milk, egg, 1 tablespoon melted butter. Mix into flour mixture until batter is fully, combined.
- In skillet over medium-low heat, heat 1 tablespoon butter. Drop batter, 1 tablespoon at a time, onto heated skillet. Cook until bubbles form, 1½ to 2 minutes. Flip and continue cooking until brown, about 1 minute more. Lay on plate lined with paper towel to help soak up excess butter. Repeat with remaining batter.

Serve

Place 1 tablespoon mushroom caviar on each blini, top with dollop of sour cream.

Entrée

Beef Stroganoff

Ingredients

- 2 pounds sirloin steak, ¼ inch thick, cut in 1-1½ inch strips
- ½ cup red wine
- ¼ cup all-purpose flour
- ¼ cup butter
- 1 onion, small, diced
- 3 cloves garlic, minced
- 2 cups mushrooms, sliced, canned
- 1 10 ounce can beef broth
- ½ cup water
- 1 tablespoon Worcestershire sauce
- 1 teaspoon salt
- 1 teaspoon paprika

- ½ teaspoon black pepper
- 2 tablespoons red pepper flakes
- 1 teaspoon yellow mustard
- ½ cup sour cream
- 2 cups egg noodles, hot, cooked

Directions

- In medium shallow bowl, mix steak, red wine, set aside to marinate 30 minutes.
- Combine flour, salt, pepper, paprika in a resealable plastic bag.
- Remove steak from marinade, reserve wine for later use, add steak to flour mixture, shake to coat.
- In large skillet, melt butter over medium-high heat. Cook, stir steak, onion, garlic until steak is browned, onion is softened, translucent, 10-15 minutes.
- Stir in mushrooms, beef broth, water, reserved red wine marinade, Worcestershire sauce, red pepper flakes, mustard until well mixed. Bring to boil. Reduce heat, cover and simmer until steak is very tender, about 1 hour. Stir sour cream into steak mixture, cook and stir until warmed 2-3 minutes.

Serve

In large shallow bowls over cooked egg noodles.

Dessert
Sharlotka

Ingredients

- 4 apples, cut in slices
- 1 cup flour
- 1 cup sugar
- 4 eggs
- 1 teaspoon baking powder

Instructions

- Preheat oven to 350°F. Grease a round 9 inch baking pan with butter. Arrange apples slices in layers in bottom of pan.
- In a large bowl, whisk eggs, sugar. Add flour, baking powder, mix until combined. Pour batter over apples. Bake for 45 minutes.

Serve

With fresh whipped cream or vanilla ice cream.

Falstaff

by Giuseppe Verdi

Commedia lirica in three acts. 1892. Libretto by Arrigo Boito, after Shakespeare's The Merry Wives of Windsor. First performance at the Teatro alla Scala, Milan, on 9th February 1893.

At the Garter Inn Falstaff quarrels with Dr Caius over an earlier drunken episode. He sends his page with love letters to Mrs. Page and Mrs. Ford who in the following scene plan their revenge together while Falstaff's follower Pistol tells Ford what is happening. Nannetta, daughter of the Fords, has a brief moment of love with Fenton. The plot against Falstaff is carried forward through Mistress Quickly who makes an appointment for him with Mrs. Ford. Ford himself appears at the inn in disguise, offering a bribe if Falstaff will pave the way for him by seducing Mrs. Ford.

Learning of the assignation already arranged, Ford is jealous. In the following scene at Ford's house, the women prepare a laundry-basket for the trick they will play on Falstaff while Mrs. Ford assures Nannetta of her opposition to her father's proposed match for her with Dr Caius. The arrival of the jealous Ford leads to Falstaff's concealment in the laundry-basket covered with dirty linen. Attention is distracted by Nannetta and Fenton behind a screen and mistaken by Ford and his band for Falstaff. The scene ends with Falstaff tipped into the river but still believing in Mrs. Ford's love for him as he is lured into a supposed assignation at midnight in Windsor Forest. There he is tormented by what he supposes to be fairies.

In the end, while Fenton and Nannetta are united and Dr Caius frustrated, Falstaff accepts what has happened stoically.

Verdi's last opera was given its first performance some six years after his earlier Shakespearean opera Otello (Othello), staged at La Scala, Milan, in February 1887. It takes the composer, now in old age, into a new world of comedy with a text that he can treat more responsively than ever. The score contains a wealth of rich invention and the opera ends with a fugue, introduced by Falstaff's Tutto nel mondo è burla (Everything in the world is a joke).

A moment of pathos may be heard in Falstaff's account of his handsome youth, Quand'ero paggio del Duca di Norfolk (When I was page to the Duke of Norfolk). Fenton's loving Del labbro il canto estasiato vola (From my lips ecstatic song takes flight) opens the final scene in Windsor Forest where Falstaff, disguised and wearing antlers, hears midnight strike, the notes striking with a fascinating harmony with each stroke of the bell.

Appetizer

Sir John's Salad

Ingredients

- 2 heads romaine lettuce
- 1 red onion, peeled, sliced in rounds, then half
- 2 tomatoes, diced
- ¼ cup mozzarella, diced
- ½ cup Extra virgin olive oil
- ¼ cup balsamic vinegar
- 1 teaspoon honey
- 1-2 teaspoon dijon mustard
- 1 teaspoon Italian seasoning
- Salt & pepper

Directions

- In large salad bowl, rip lettuce in bite size pieces.

- Add onion, tomatoes, mozzarella to lettuce.
- Whisk together rest of ingredients, pour over salad, toss.

Entree
Falstaff's Fig and Prosciutto Penne

Based on the rich fruit sauces popular in the Renaissance and Elizabethan eras. It may have even been on the bill of fare at the Garter's Inn! Figs and prosciutto, a classic Italian combination, make a delicious pasta topping. Dried figs simmered with wine and stock take on a delightful, complex flavor with pleasing firmness. The silky-sweet fig sauce is tossed with penne and then accented with luscious prosciutto and crunchy pistachios. Their sweetness is balanced with the piquant bite of pink peppercorn and the salty goodness of Parmesan.

Ingredients
- ½ cup butter
- 2 tablespoons extra virgin olive oil
- 6 shallots, sliced
- 1 cup white wine
- 16 to 18 dried Calimyrna figs, approximately 12 ounces, thinly sliced
- 1½ cups chicken stock
- 1 pound penne
- ¼ pound prosciutto di Parma, sliced paper thin
- ½ cup parmesan cheese, shaved
- ¼ cup pistachio nuts, coarsely crushed
- 1 tablespoon whole pink peppercorns

Directions
- In medium saucepan, add wine, figs, simmer until wine is absorbed, figs are soft, about 8 minutes.
- Stir in stock, simmer, covered for about 7 minutes.

Remove from heat.

- Prepare penne according to package directions. Drain, toss with fig sauce.

Serve

- Top penne with prosciutto, parmesan, pistachio nuts, pink peppercorns.

Dessert
Aniseed Cake

Ingredients

- 2 eggs, separated
- ⅔ cup sugar
- 1 cup flour
- 3 tablespoons aniseed, crushed
- Icing sugar

Directions

- Preheat oven to 325°F.
- In medium bowl, beat egg yolks with sugar until pale yellow. In separate medium bowl, beat egg whites until stiff. Sift flour, aniseed into egg yolk mixture. Stir in egg whites until just combined, do not over stir.
- Pour in a tube or bundt pan. Bake for 40 mins, check at 30 mins, cake is cooked when springs back to touch. Let cool, then turn out on cooling rack. When cool dust top with icing sugar.

Halka

by Stanislaw Moniuszko

*Part of the canon **of** Polish national operas. Libretto by Włodzimierz Wolski, a young Warsaw poet with radical social views. The first performance of two-act version, a concert performance in Vilnius on 1 January 1848. Staged premiere in same city 28 February 1854. A four-act version was performed in Warsaw on 1 January 1858.*

Guests at an engagement party are happy the wedding of Janusz, a wealthy young landowner, to Zofia the daughter of an even wealthier landowner named Stolnik will unite two huge estates. Zofia and Janusz celebrate a toast with Stolnik, and Stolnik calls Janusz the son he has always wanted. The party is disturbed by a plaintive wailing from outside. It seems to be a troubled young girl crying for her lost love. The kind-hearted Zofia asks Janusz to talk to the girl hoping he will comfort her. He reluctantly agrees. Dziemba, the steward of Stolnik's estate, ushers in the woebegone creature.

To the audience's surprise, she appears to know Janusz. He himself is her lost love and promised her marriage while in her village in the mountains but then disappeared. As soon as Halka looks into Janusz's eyes she is convinced that his feelings for her haven't changed despite the disquieting rumours she had heard to the contrary.

Halka throws her arms around Janusz and he says that he still loves her as he did before. He tells Halka to meet him after dark at the statue of the Virgin Mary by the river They will escape together to start a new life somewhere else. Once Halka goes out Janusz returns to the party. Halka is waiting for Janusz by the river.

She is disturbed by the appearance of not Janusz but Jontek, a friend from her mountain village. Jontek has been in unrequited love with Halka for many years. Halka tells him happily that Janusz still loves her but Jontek insists that she has been betrayed. Jontek can't convince Halka until he drags her to the scene of the party, where she sees that Janusz has become engaged to Zofia. Halka is devastated and compares herself to a dove who has been ripped to pieces by a falcon.

Act 3 opens with happy scenes of normal life back in Halka's mountain village. The villagers are dismayed by the arrival of Jontek and an unrecognizable woman, who turns out to be the saddened Halka. They are angry when they hear about Janusz's engagement and even angrier when they realize that Halka is pregnant. Halka is in a world of her own, crushed by grief and fixated on the images of the dove being broken by the falcon. A black raven passes overhead boding ill for everyone. Jontek is very sad about Halka.

When a piper in the village to play at the wedding of Janusz and Zofia appears playing a happy tune, Jontek asks him what there is to be so happy about. The piper mollifies him by playing a haunting mountain song. Jontek describes his love for Halka and the many wonders of nature she reminds him of.

When Janusz and Zofia arrive in the village to celebrate their wedding, the angry villagers have to be convinced to act festive by Dziemba, the steward, who persuades them to do so out of respect for the bride. Zofia notices that Halka is terribly upset. She thinks she has seen Halka somewhere before, and even asks her what's wrong. Janusz admits that Halka is the girl who interrupted their engagement party but whisks Zofia into the church before she can ask any more questions.

Halka is heartbroken to see that Janusz is going through with the marriage. She has lost her baby and feels completely alone. In a fit of rage, she decides to burn down the church. However, she decides to let Janusz live and throws herself into the river instead.

Appetizer
Bigos
Hunter's Stew

Bigos is considered a Polish national dish, which, according to American food historian William Woys Weaver, "has been romanticized in poetry, discussed in its most minute details in all sorts of literary contexts, and never made in small quantities."

Ingredients
- 4 slices chickory smoked bacon
- 2 yellow onions, chopped
- 1 pound Polish sausage, quartered
- 1 pound beef or pork stew meat
- 2 cups wild mushrooms, sliced
- 4-5 large garlic cloves
- 3-4 medium carrots, diced
- 1½ pound drained sauerkraut (do not rinse)
- 5 cups cabbage, shredded
- 1 cup chopped prunes
- 1½ teaspoons dried thyme
- 1½ teaspoons dried marjoram
- 1 teaspoon allspice
- 1 large bay leaf
- 2 tablespoons sweet paprika
- 1 teaspoon caraway seeds, crushed
- Cayenne pepper, pinch
- 1 cup dry red wine

- 4 cups beef stock
- 1 can diced tomatoes, optional
- Mushroom powder, optional
- Salt & pepper to taste

Directions

- In large stock pot, saute onions, bacon on medium heat, cover. Stir occasionally until onions start to brown. Add mushrooms, cook until soft. Do not crisp bacon. Add sausage, beef or pork, mixing until brown. Add remaining ingredients (except prunes), if there is not enough room, add the cabbage first to reduce.
- Saute 2-3 hours on low heat. Cook until liquid is reduced, stew thickens. Stir every 20 minutes. Add more red wine or broth if dry.

Helpful Hint

If you need more fat, add olive oil. Do not overcook meat, just brown on outside. Use good smoked Polish sausage, will not need to brown very long.

Bigos should always be juicy. Add more paprika or pepper if needed but flavor will develop overnight.

Serve

Mix thoroughly, heat with prunes for 10 minutes until soft. Serve with rye bread.

Entree
Potato Cheese Pierogi

Traditionally considered peasant food, pierogi eventually gained popularity and spread throughout all social classes including nobles. Some cookbooks from the 17th century describe how during that era the pierogi were considered a staple of the Polish diet and each holiday had its own special kind of pierogi created. Different shapes and fillings were made for holidays such as Christmas and Easter.

Perogi were made especially for mourning's or wakes and some for caroling season in January.

Ingredients
- 4½ cups all-purpose flour
- 2 teaspoons salt
- 2 tablespoons butter, melted
- 2 cups sour cream
- 2 eggs
- 1 egg yolk
- 2 tablespoons vegetable oil
- 8 baking potatoes, peeled, cubed
- 1 cup cheddar cheese, shredded
- 2 tablespoons processed cheese sauce
- Onion salt to taste, optional
- Salt & pepper to taste

Directions
- In large bowl, stir together flour, salt. In separate bowl, whisk together butter, sour cream, eggs, egg yolk, oil.
- Stir wet ingredients into flour, salt until well blended. Cover bowl with towel, let stand 15-20 minutes.
- In large saucepan, place potatoes in pot, fill with enough water to cover. Bring to boil, cook until tender, approximately 15 minutes.
- Drain, mash with shredded cheese, cheese sauce while hot. Season with onion salt, salt & pepper. Set aside to cool.
- Separate pierogi dough into two balls. Roll out one piece at a time on lightly floured surface until thin enough to work with, but not too thin so that it tears.
- Cut into circles using a cookie cutter, pierogi cutter or glass. Brush a little water around edges of circles, spoon some filling into center. Fold circles over half-

circles, press to seal edges. Place perogies on a cookie sheet, freeze. Once frozen, transfer to freezer storage bags or containers.

- To cook perogies: Bring a large pot of lightly salted water to a boil. Drop perogies in one at a time. They are done when they float to the top. Do not overboil, remove with a slotted spoon.

Dessert
Apple Strudel with Vanilla Sauce

Ingredients
- 1 egg
- 2 tablespoons granulated sugar
- 3 tablespoons all-purpose flour
- ¼ teaspoon ground cinnamon
- 2 large granny smith apples, peeled, cored, thinly sliced
- 2 tablespoons raisins
- ½ of 17.3 oz package of puff pastry sheets, thawed
- 1 tablespoon confectioner's sugar

Directions
- Preheat oven to 375°F. In small bowl, beat egg, water with fork.
- In medium bowl stir granulated sugar, 1 tablespoon flour, cinnamon. Add apples, raisins, toss to coat
- Sprinkle remaining flour on work surface. Unfold pastry sheet, roll into 16 x 12-inch rectangle. With short side facing you, spoon apple mixture on bottom half of sheet to 1 inch of edge, roll up like a jelly roll. Place seam-side down onto baking sheet, tuck ends under to seal.
- Brush pastry with egg mixture. Cut 4 deep slits in top of pastry. Bake 35 minutes or until golden brown. Let cool on baking sheet on wire rack for 20 minutes. Sprinkle with confectioners' sugar.

Vanilla Sauce

Ingredients

- ¾ cup milk
- ½ cup light cream
- ⅓ cup sugar
- 4 egg yolks, beaten
- ½ vanilla bean

Directions

- In 2-quart saucepan, add all ingredients. Cook and stir over medium heat until mixture boils and thickens.
- Remove saucepan from heat, cover, refrigerate 1 hour. Remove vanilla bean.

Helpful Hints

For nutty crunch, add ¼ cup sliced almonds with the apples and raisins.

To thicken the juices released by the apples as they cook, toss apples and raisins until evenly coated with flour mixture.

For Pear and Cranberry Strudel, substitute pears and dried cranberries for the apples and raisins.

Il Trovatore

by Giuseppe Verdi

Drama four parts. First performed in 1853. Libretto by Salvadore Cammarano, completed by Leone Emanuele Bardare, after the play El trovador (The Troubadour) by Antonio García Gutiérrez. First performance at the Teatro Apollo, Rome on 19th January 1853.

The four parts of the opera have the titles The Duel, The Gypsy, The Gypsy's Son and The Execution. Ferrando tells the story of the revenge taken by a gypsy for the death of her mother, the apparent destruction in the fire of the son of the old Count di Luna. In the palace gardens Leonora waits for her lover, the troubadour Manrico, mistaking the Count di Luna, who also loves her for him, an error that ends with a duel between the two men.

At the gypsy camp Azucena tells Manrico the story of the abduction of the son of the Count di Luna and admits that she threw the wrong baby on the fire, keeping, as her own, the Count's son. He tells her how he was held back from killing the young Count in their duel. News comes that Leonora, thinking Manrico dead, is to enter a convent, a step that the Count seeks to prevent. The arrival of Manrico with his men allows him to take Leonora away with him.

Azucena is captured by the Count's men who are preparing to attack Castellor, Manrico's stronghold. In the castle the planned marriage of Manrico and Leonora is interrupted by news of Azucena's capture. Imprisoned by the Count, Manrico and Azucena are threatened with death. Leonora seeks to save her lover, offering herself in return, although she has secretly taken poison.

In the prison Azucena reveals to Manrico his parentage, as a son of the old Count and brother to his enemy. Leonora comes to bring news of Manrico's release and dies. The Count orders the immediate execution of Manrico, watched by Azucena, who has her final triumphant revenge when she reveals to the Count the identity of his victim.

Il Trovatore (The Troubadour) followed close upon the success of Verdi's Rigoletto and was to be followed by La traviata (The Fallen Woman). It retains its place as a major element in Italian opera repertoire in spite of the improbabilities of a plot in which Azucena might seem to have suffered a confusion of mind worthy of Miss Prism. This lack of verisimilitude is forgotten in the dramatic strength of the music. Ferrando's narrative, Di due figli vivea padre felice (There lived once a happy father of two boys) sets the opening.

The second scene allows Leonora her Tacea la notte placida (Silent was the night), as she tells Ines of when she first heard Manrico's serenade, Deserto sulla terra (Deserted on the earth).

The second act starts with the famous Anvil Chorus, Vedi! Le fosche notturne (See! The darkness of night goes) as the gypsies in their encampment start their day, a chorus that has its third part parallel in the song of the Count's soldiers, Or co' dadi (Now we gamble). The second act also brings Azucena's powerful account of her mother's death, Stride la vampa (The fire roars).

She has her moments again when she is interrogated by the Count, as his prisoner, Giorni poveri vivea (There in poverty) and Deh! Rallentate o barbari (Ah! Cruel men, loosen these chains), and in her final scene with Manrico.

For Leonora herself there is the moving D'amor sull'ali rosee (Love, fly on rosy wings) as she hears the Miserere from within the castle where Manrico is held prisoner and her final scene with Manrico.

Appetizer
Gypsy Soup

Ingredients

- 4 tablespoons olive oil
- 2 large onions, chopped
- 2 stalks celery, chopped
- 2 cloves garlic, crushed
- 3 medium sweet potatoes, diced, peeled
- 1 teaspoon paprika
- ½ teaspoon ground turmeric
- ½ teaspoon dried basil
- 1 teaspoon salt
- 1 pinch ground cinnamon
- 1 pinch cayenne pepper
- 1 bay leaf
- 3 cups chicken stock
- 3 teaspoons tamari
- 2 medium tomatoes, chopped
- 1 14 ounce can garbanzo beans
- 1 medium green bell pepper, chopped

Directions

- Heat oil in stock pot over medium-high heat. Saute onion, garlic, celery, sweet potatoes for 5 minutes until onion is soft. Season with paprika, turmeric, basil, salt, cinnamon, cayenne, bay leaf, stir to blend.
- Stir in chicken stock, tamari, cover and simmer on low heat for 15 minutes. Add tomatoes, garbanzo beans, green pepper, simmer for another 10 minutes until

vegetables are tender. Salt & pepper to taste.

Entrée
Chicken Mushroom Cobbler with Gruyere Herb Biscuits

Ingredients

- 3 cups mushrooms of your choice, sliced
- 2 cups mini potatoes, halved
- 2 tablespoons olive oil
- 1 teaspoon fresh thyme, chopped
- 1 teaspoon fresh rosemary, chopped
- 2 chicken breasts, skin on, cooked or 2 cups cooked chicken, cubed
- 1 onion, diced
- 1 leek, halved, chopped
- 1½ tablespoons butter
- 1½ tablespoons flour
- 3 cups chicken stock, cold
- ¼ cup light cooking cream

Gruyere Herb Biscuits

Ingredients

- 2 cups flour
- 4 teaspoons baking powder
- ½ teaspoon salt
- 1 teaspoon fresh rosemary, chopped
- 1 teaspoon fresh thyme, chopped
- ½ cup butter, cold, cut in 1 inch cubes
- ⅔ cup milk
- 1 cup gruyere cheese, grated
- 2 teaspoons light cooking cream, 15% milk fat

For Cobbler:

- Preheat oven to 350°F. Coat 8 cup casserole dish or 8 inch cast iron pan well with oil. In large saute pan, saute mushrooms in olive oil over medium-high heat until golden brown, remove from pan, reserve in casserole dish.

- In medium saucepan, while mushrooms are on, add mini-potatoes, cover with water, cook until just tender. Cool immediately in cold water, drain well, reserve with mushrooms. Add cubed chicken mix to combine evenly. This is your cobbler 'base'.
- In saute pan used for mushrooms, add oil if needed, saute onions, leeks over medium heat until transparent. When onions are cooked, but not browned, add butter, melt, stirring occasionally. Add flour, stirring well to combine, coat. Add cream, herbs. Reduce for 8-10 minutes on low simmer to thicken.
- Taste, season, pour sauce over cobbler base, mix.

Helpful Hint

This is a basic roux, cook 3-4 minutes to cook flour before adding chicken stock to deglaze.

For Biscuits:
- Pre-heat oven to 350°F.
- In food processor, add dry ingredients; flour, baking powder, salt & herbs, pulse twice to combine.
- Add half butter, pulse 3-4 times, repeat with remaining butter until coarse dry meal, size of a small pea.
- Transfer to large bowl, add milk, gruyere, mix with wooden spoon to form a dry dough. Turn dough out onto lightly floured, clean counter-top, knead about 90 seconds to form a smooth dough.
- Cut, rip, drop dough on top of casserole or form a lid over the base with a continuous sheet of biscuit dough on top of the casserole base, leaving a ½ inch gap around the edge. Brush biscuit top with cream, bake 35–45 minutes until golden brown and bubbling.

Helpful Hint
If you lack the fancy food processor, use a bowl, freeze the butter and grate it in. Same result, less dishes.
Make ahead of time and store in refrigerator until needed.

Dessert
Strawberry Gypsy Pie

Ingredients
- 2½ cups all purpose flour
- ¾ cup unsalted butter, cold, cut into cubes
- ½ teaspoon salt
- 4-6 tablespoons ice water
- ¼ cup cornstarch
- ¼ teaspoon salt
- 1 cup sugar
- 2 pounds strawberries, ripe, stemmed, not sliced
- 1 egg, beaten
- 1 teaspoon orange peel, grated

Directions
- Preheat oven to 350°F. In medium bowl, blend flour, butter, salt with fingertips. Drizzle 4-6 tablespoons ice water evenly over, stir until incorporated. Turn dough out on work surface, divide into 2 portions. Gently shape into two disks, wrap separately in plastic wrap, chill until firm, at least 1 hour.
- Remove one from refrigerator, let sit at room temperature 5-10 minutes to soften to make rolling out easier. Roll out with rolling pin on lightly floured surface. Carefully place onto a pie plate. Trim dough.
- Mix strawberries, sugar, cornstarch, salt, orange rind, let sit for 10 minutes. Add filling to pie.
- Roll out second disk of dough, as before. Gently place on top of filling in pie. Pinch top, bottom of dough rounds firmly together. Fold edge of top piece over and

under edge of bottom piece, pressing together. Brush top of pie with beaten egg. Cut three steam vents in top crust with small, sharp knife.

- Bake for 20 minutes, reduce heat to 300°F, bake additional 30-40 minutes until crust is golden brown. Cool pie on rack at least 2 hours before serving.

La Boheme

by Giacomo Puccini

Opera in four acts. 1895.Libretto by Giuseppe Giacosa and Luigi Illica, after the novel Scène de la vie de bohème (Scene of Bohemian Life) by Henri Murger. First performance at the Teatro Regio, Turin, on 1st February 1896.

In an attic apartment in the Latin Quarter of Paris a group of young artists are living together in poverty. Their neighbour, the little seamstress Mimi, introduces herself seeking a light for her candle when Rodolfo is left alone. They fall in love. At the Café Momus Rodolfo presents Mimi to his friends while the singer Musetta abandons her elderly rich lover Alcindoro in order to join Marcello. Alcindoro is left to settle the bill for all of them. Time has passed. Mimi has lived with Rodolfo, but they quarrel because of his apparent jealousy. He has planned to leave her as we learn in a scene set on a cold winter morning by the city gates.

Musetta, a contrast in character to the gentle Mimi, later returns to the attic apartment of the four young men. She brings the dying Mimi with her, whom they now try to comfort in vain, as she dies before their eyes of the consumption that has racked her.

Ruggero Leoncavallo claimed priority in his own operatic version of La Bohème with a libretto of his own devising based on the novel by Murger. His version was first performed on 6th May 1897 at the Teatro La Fenice, Venice and won immediate if not lasting success of the same degree as Puccini's opera. The latter version is among the best known of all works in the current repertoire, a thoroughly romantic treatment, with an element of realism in its setting.

The score has provided singers with operatic recital repertoire, in particular the tenor Che gelida manina (Your tiny hand is frozen), Mimi's Mi chiamano Mimi (They call me Mimi), Rodolfo's O soave fanciulla (O sweet girl) and Musetta's Waltz.

Appetizer
Cheese Fondue

Ingredients

- 1¼ pounds Comté, Gruyère or Emmental cheese, shredded
- 3 tablespoons all purpose flour
- 1 garlic clove, halved
- 1½ cups dry white wine, unoaked Chardonnay or Sauvignon Blanc
- ½ teaspoon nutmeg, or to taste
- ¼ cup whole milk, if needed
- Toasted baguette bread cubes
- Pears, apples, sliced
- Ground black pepper
- Fondue pot

Directions

- Bring cheese to room temperature, about 30 minutes. In medium size bowl, toss cheese with flour. Rub interior of fondue pot with garlic clove.
- In medium-size saucepan over medium heat, heat wine to low simmer. Add cheese by the handful, stirring with wooden spoon until melted before adding more. Stir in nutmeg, season to taste with pepper. If fondue is too thick stir in a little milk, up to ¼ cup.
- Transfer to fondue pot, keep bubbling gently over fondue burner, following the manufacturer's directions.

Serve

With toasted bread cubes, apple, pear slices.

Entree
Chicken Marengo

Ingredients

- 1 cup crayfish tails or shrimp
- 1 whole chicken, cut up
- 1 large onion, peeled, chopped
- 1 clove of garlic, crushed
- 6 tomatoes, chopped
- 6 tablespoons brandy or dry sherry
- 2 tablespoons plain flour
- Handful of torn basil leaves
- 3 tablespoons black olives, optional
- 2 Free range eggs to garnish, optional but authentic!
- Salt & pepper to taste

Directions

- Season flour with salt & pepper. Roll the chicken pieces in the flour.
- In large pot, heat olive oil, brown chicken pieces, 3 minutes each side, remove and keep warm.
- Add onion and garlic and more olive oil if needed until onion softens. Add chicken back to the pan. Add tomatoes, brandy, cover and simmer on low heat for 30 minutes. Add crayfish tails, simmer for a further 10 minutes.
- At the last minute, stir in basil leaves, olives.

Serve

Fry eggs, serve as garnish.
Serve with crusty bread.

Dessert
Profiteroles

Ingredients

- 1 cup water
- ½ cup butter
- ¼ teaspoon salt

- 1 cup all-purpose flour
- 4 eggs

Directions

- Preheat oven to 425°F. Line baking sheet with parchment paper.
- Bring water to a boil in saucepan, stir in butter and salt until melted, remove from heat. Stir in flour until smooth, stir in eggs one at a time.
- Drop evenly spaced dollops of profiterole paste onto prepared baking sheet. Bake 25-30 minutes until pastries puff up and turn golden brown. Cool on wire rack to room temperature.

Warm Chocolate Sauce

Ingredients

- 2 cups heavy cream
- ¼ cup confectioners' sugar
- 1 teaspoon rose water, optional
- 9 ounces semisweet chocolate, chopped

Directions

- Beat 1 cup heavy cream to soft peaks, stir in confectioners' sugar until dissolved.
- Simmer remaining cup of heavy cream in small saucepan over medium heat, remove from heat, stir in chocolate until melted and smooth

Serve

Cut each pastry in half, fill with cream. Place filled profiteroles on individual serving plates, top with warm chocolate sauce.

La Traviata

by Giuseppe Verdi

*Opera in three acts. 1853. Libretto by Francesco Maria Piave,
after the play La Dame aux camélias (The Lady of the Camelias) by
Alexandre Dumas fils. First performance at the Teatro La Fenice,
Venice on 6th March 1853.*

At a party in her house, Violetta is moved to learn that the young Alfredo Germont is in love with her. There are however hints that she is suffering from consumption. They set up house together in the country but Violetta secretly sells her jewels to meet the expenses they now incur. Alfredo learns of this from Violetta's maid Annina and goes to Paris to raise money. In his absence, his father arrives seeking to persuade Violetta to leave Alfredo whose behavior prejudices the marriage chances of his sister as well as his own prospects.

Violetta sacrifices her own feelings and accepts an invitation from her friend Flora Bervoix which will take her back to her old life, now under the protection of Baron Douphol. She leaves a note for Alfredo telling him of her decision while old Germont tries to comfort his son without revealing anything of Violetta's true motives. Alfredo then bursts into the party at Flora's house and insults Violetta whom he finds with her new protector. She falls back fainting as the second act closes. In the third act Violetta is at home near to death. Germont has told his son of the sacrifice she had made and Alfredo now returns holding her in his arms as she dies.

La Traviata is one of those operas that has retained a firm position in current repertoire never failing in its effect.

The prelude to the first act uses the tender and melancholy music that later precedes Violetta's death as well as Violetta's plea to Alfredo to love her. The music preceding Violetta's death returns in the prelude to the Third Act. At Violetta's there is a lively drinking-song or brindisi, Libiamo (Let us drink) led by Alfredo and as the guests go into the next room he declares his love for her in Un dì felice (One happy day). Her response to his declarations is heard in her later reflective Ah, fors'è lui (Ah perhaps it is he my heart desires). In the second act Alfredo considers the happiness that life with Violetta has brought him in De' miei bollenti spiriti (Fervent my dream of ecstasy).

Germont's attempts to remind his son of their home, Di Provenza il mar, il suol (The sea, the land of Provence) have provided baritones with a moving aria and there is later contrast in the masquerading gypsy and Spanish dances at the house of Flora Bervoix. Although set in 1700 it could have a contemporary setting and relevance in the Paris of the 1850s. An element of realism less apparent in operas drawing, according to tradition, on the historical activities of kings and princes.

Appetizer
Minestrone alla Traviata

This is one of the best soups you'll ever taste. Fresh tomatoes contribute to a big part of the soup's flavor. They are only cooked a short time, so you really savor true tomato taste. Halve the tomatoes on a cutting board, drop into boiling water and the skins fall off by themselves.

Try and use fresh tomatoes, even top-quality canned tomatoes do not approach the flavor of fresh heirloom or vine-ripened tomatoes. The dish is a soup version of pasta puttanesca and would have been a fitting first course at one of Violetta's fine dinner parties.

Ingredients
- 2 tablespoons Extra virgin olive oil
- 1 large red onion, minced
- 2 anchovy fillets, mashed
- 6 garlic cloves, minced
- ½ cup white wine
- 2 cups vegetable or chicken stock
- 6 to 7 heirloom tomatoes, peeled, seeded, chopped
- 20 oil-cured black olives, pitted, coarsely chopped
- 1 tablespoon capers, drained
- Red pepper flakes
- Parsley, chopped, for serving
- Romano cheese, grated, for serving
- Salt & fresh black pepper

Directions
- Heat oil in medium saucepan over medium-low heat, add onion, cook 10 minutes until soft. Add anchovy, garlic, red pepper flakes to taste, wine, bring to boil. Add stock, tomatoes, return to boil, quickly remove from heat to cool.
- Transfer to food processor, puree until smooth.
- Return to saucepan, stir in olives, capers, season to taste with salt & pepper.

Serve
Reheat the soup on low until warm, serve topped with parsley, sprinkle of Romano cheese.

Entree
Boneless Pork Roast with Vegetables
Ingredients
- 4-5 pounds boneless pork loin
- 1 tablespoon garlic powder
- 1 tablespoon onion powder
- 1 tablespoon parsley
- 1 tablespoon rosemary
- 1 tablespoon seasoning salt
- 1 tablespoon Extra virgin olive oil
- 1 teaspoon black pepper
- 10 fresh garlic cloves, chopped
- 5-6 yukon gold potatoes, quartered
- 8-16 ounces baby carrots
- 1 large onion, quartered
- 1 8 ounce can beef broth

Directions
- Preheat oven to 325°F.
- Place pork loin fat side up in large pan, arrange vegetables around it.
- In small bowl mix garlic powder, onion powder, seasoned salt, black pepper, rub on top of pork.
- Sprinkle pork and vegetables with parsley, garlic, drizzle olive oil, add additional seasoning to vegetables if desired. Add beef broth in one of the corners of the pan, do not pour over pork.
- Place foil, slightly vented, over the pork, fitting the pan. Cook 2½ hours.
- To brown, after it's done, remove foil, turn broiler to high, broil meat side up 10 minutes, fat side up 10 minutes, repeat twice and one additional meat side up for final 10 minutes, check browning throughout.
- Remove from oven, let meat rest for 30 minutes.

Dessert
Poached Pears in Spiced Brown Sugar Syrup

Ingredients

- 1 vanilla bean, halved lengthways
- 2 cinnamon sticks
- ¼ teaspoon ground nutmeg
- 2 cups firmly packed brown sugar
- 4 bosc pears, peeled
- Double cream or ice-cream, to serve

Directions

- Place 4 cups cold water, vanilla, cinnamon, nutmeg, sugar in saucepan over medium-high heat, bring to boil, reduce heat to medium-low.
- Add pears, cook partially covered, turning occasionally 18 to 20 minutes until pears are just tender. Remove from heat. Let pears cool in syrup, turning occasionally. Using a slotted spoon, transfer pears to a plate.
- Return syrup to medium-high heat, bring to boil for 10 minutes until liquid is reduced by one-third.

Serve

- Serve pears with sugar syrup and cream or ice-cream.

Madame Butterfly

by Giacomo Puccini

*Tragedia giapponese in two acts. 1903. Libretto by Giuseppe Giacosa
and Luigi Illica, after the play Madame Butterfly by David Belasco,
based on John Luther Long's story, a work indebted to Pierre Loti's
Madame Chrysanthème. First performance at the Teatro alla Scala,
Milan, on 28th May 1904*

Goro the marriage-broker shows Lieutenant Pinkerton the
house where he will live with Cio-Cio-San after their marriage
and introduces the servants. Pinkerton explains to the consul
Sharples, who has joined him, that he has the house on a long
lease to be terminated at a month's notice. His coming
marriage is to be undertaken on similar terms since he has no
intention of continuing the relationship.

Cio-Cio-San and her family arrive and the wedding takes
place interrupted by the Bonze who curses her as a renegade.
As evening draws on the company disperses eaving Cio-Cio-
San and Pinkerton alone together. Three years later she still
awaits the return of Pinkerton who has never seen the son she
has borne him. Attempts are made by Goro to bring about
another marriage to Prince Yamadori. Eventually Pinkerton
does return having prepared Sharpless by a letter. He brings
with him his American wife to retrieve the child and Cio-Cio-
San kills herself with the knife that her father had used for his
own death by imperial command.

Madama Butterfly is one of Puccini's most moving operas.
Japanese melodies are used to provide an element of
authenticity with American musical references to mark
Pinkerton's primary loyalties.

Its drama centred on Cio-Cio-San whose childish innocence at her marriage and continued ingenuous faith are contrasted with the callousness of Pinkerton.

There is a fine extended love duet for Cio-Cio-San and Pinkerton at the end of the first act, Viene la sera (Evening approaches) with her later Un bel dì vedremo (One fine day we shall see) among the best known of all Italian operatic arias. As Pinkerton's ship returns she and Suzuki decorate the house with cherry-blossom, Scuoti quella fronda di ciliegio (Shake that cherry-tree branch), while the Humming Chorus provides an interlude before Pinkerton's delayed appearance for which she has waited so long. He feels a touch of sorrow at what he has done, as he bids the little house farewell in Addio, fiorito asil (Farewell, happy home).

Appetizer
Miso Soup

Ingredients
- ½ cup dried wakame (seaweed)
- ¼ cup shiro miso (white fermented-soybean paste)
- 6 cups warm water
- ½ pound soft tofu, drained, cut in ½ inch cubes
- ¼ cup scallion greens, thinly sliced

Directions
- Cover wakame with 1 inch warm water, let stand 15 minutes to reconstitute, drain in sieve.
- Stir together miso, ½ cup water until smooth.
- Heat remaining water in saucepan over moderate-high heat until hot, gently stir in tofu and wakame. Simmer 1 minute, remove from heat.

Serve
Stir miso mixture into tofu mixture. To with scallion greens.

Entree
Roasted Orange Chicken

Ingredients

- 8 5-ounce skinless chicken breast halves, with bone
- 1 cup orange marmalade
- 1 tablespoon reduced-sodium soy sauce
- 1 teaspoon liquid smoke
- Salt & ground black pepper

Directions

- Preheat oven to 400°F. Coat a large roasting pan with cooking spray.
- Season chicken with salt & ground black pepper, arrange chicken in pan.
- In small bowl, combine orange marmalade, soy sauce, liquid smoke, mix until blended, pour mixture over chicken.
- Roast 35 minutes, until chicken is cooked through.

Side Dish
Stir Fried Vegetable Rice

Ingredients

- 4 cups cooked white rice, make day before, refrigerate
- 2 tablespoons vegetable or canola oil, divided
- 1 bag frozen Japanese stir fry vegetables
- 2 scallions, thinly sliced
- 2 medium cloves garlic, minced
- 2 teaspoon soy sauce
- 1 teaspoon toasted sesame oil, optional
- 1 large egg
- Ground white pepper

Directions

- Break rice up into small grains, heat ½ tablespoon vegetable oil in large wok or frypan over high heat until smoking.

- Add half of rice, cook, stir and toss until rice is pale brown, toasted with chewy texture, about three minutes. Transfer to medium bowl. Repeat with another ½ tablespoon oil, remaining rice.
- Return all rice to wok, press to sides leaving space in middle.
- Add ½ tablespoon oil to space, scallions, garlic and cook, stirring gently, until lightly softened about 1 minute. Toss with rice to combine.
- Add soy sauce, sesame oil, toss to coat. Salt and white pepper to taste. Push rice to side of wok.
- Add remaining ½ tablespoon oil. Break egg into oil, season lightly with salt. Use a spatula to scramble the egg, toss egg, rice together.
- Add frozen vegetables, continue to toss, stir until thawed and every grain of rice is separate.

Dessert
Fruit Sando

Ingredients
- 6 slices regular white sliced bread, crusts removed
- 1 cup heavy whipping cream
- 2 tablespoons granulated sugar
- Fresh fruit of your choice, sliced

Directions
- Remove crusts from bread.
- In medium bowl, whip cream, sugar until stiff, soft peaks. Spread each slice of bread with whipped cream.
- Top with fruit, second slice of bread, repeat with remaining slices.
- Place in refrigerator for 20 mins.

Serve

Slice from corner to corner. Serve on plate, small edge down revealing fruit and cream.

Marriage of Figaro

by Wolfgang Amadeus Mozart

Opera buffa in four acts. 1786. Libretto by Lorenzo Da Ponte, after the play La Folle Journée, ou Le Mariage de Figaro (The Mad Day, or The Marriage of Figaro) by Pierre-Augustin Beaumarchais. First performance at the Burgtheater, Vienna, on 1st May 1786.

Figaro and Susanna are to marry but the Count has given them rooms near to his own which will be convenient if he needs access to Susanna. Bartolo wants to take revenge on Figaro who had helped the Count to marry his ward Rosina, now the Countess. His housekeeper Marcellina has lent money to Figaro who has promised to marry her if he cannot repay it. Cherubino tells Susanna that he loves all women and Susanna hides him behind a chair as the Count is heard approaching. His proposals to Susanna are interrupted by the sound of Don Basilio coming near. He too hides behind the chair allowing Cherubino to hide himself sitting on it, under a dress thrown over him by Susanna.

Basilio now refers to Cherubino's love for the Countess and the Count emerges to find out more. Susanna tries to distract them by fainting but Cherubino is discovered. Figaro brings in a group of peasants, singing praise of the Count who has surrendered his droit de seigneur (the alleged right of a medieval lord to have relations with subordinate women on her wedding night) as far as Susanna is concerned but the Count delays their marriage and packs Cherubino off to the army. Figaro, however, detains Cherubino, since he has plans for him.

In the second act the Countess, in her room, is sad, neglected by her husband.

She listens to Figaro's plan to dress Cherubino as a girl and put him in Susanna's place in an attempt to trap the Count.

Cherubino is singing of his love for the Countess when the Count returns from hunting eager to pursue matters divulged to him in an anonymous letter accusing the Countess. Cherubino hides in the closet and Susanna, unseen by the others, comes in. The Countess tells her husband that Susanna is in the closet but the door cannot be opened. The Count, suspicious, goes to fetch tools to open the door taking the Countess with him. This allows Cherubino to jump out of the window and Susanna to take his place. The Count returns and the closet is opened, revealing Susanna.

Antonio the gardener adds complications when he comes in to complain of someone jumping out of the window and Figaro now claims that it was him. The act ends with the appearance of Don Basilio, Bartolo and Marcellina, seeking justice. As the wedding is in the third act, Susanna, at the suggestion of the Countess agrees to an assignation with the Count. Marcellina's complaint against Figaro is heard and he claims that he needs parental consent for his marriage to her if it is to take place. It then transpires that Marcellina is in fact his mother and Bartolo his father. In the fourth act, in the garden at night, Figaro is given cause for jealousy of Susanna but she is now disguised as the Countess and the Countess as Susanna.

The Count unknowingly woos his own wife, while Figaro deliberately provokes his jealousy by his own approaches to the supposed Countess, which is in fact Susanna. The opera ends with the Count humbled but penitent, reconciled now with his wife, Figaro with Susanna, Cherubino with Barbarina, and Marcellina with Bartolo.

The complexities and symmetries of situation in Le nozze di Figaro make up one of the most perfect of Mozart's operas with a score that offers music of great variety admirably suited to each situation and character.

There is a brilliantly devised overture followed by the scene in which Figaro measures the room that is to be his and Susanna's. Resolving to get the better of the Count, Figaro sings his well-known Se vuol ballare, signor contino (If you want to dance, little master count). Revenge of another kind is envisaged by Bartolo in his patter-song La vendetta (Vengeance).

Cherubino opens his heart to Susanna in Non sò più cosa son, cosa faccio (I no longer know who I am or what I am doing), and when Cherubino is duly banished with an army commission Figaro mocks him with Non più andrai farfallone amoroso (You are no longer an amorous butterfly).

There is great poignancy in the Countess's second-act aria Porgi amor (Love, grant me comfort) to which perhaps Cherubino's adolescent Voi che sapete (You who know what love is) might provide consolation. The opera continues with a wealth of musical invention and apt dramatic sense. Shown to perfection in the comic finales, those final ensembles which offer either a problem to be solved or in the end a final reconciliation.

Appetizer
Italian Wedding Soup

Ingredients
- 8 ounce ground beef
- 8 ounce ground pork
- 1 teaspoon garlic, minced
- 1 teaspoon salt
- ¼ cup bread crumbs

- ½ cup grated Parmesan cheese, optional
- 12 cups chicken broth
- 1 box frozen spinach, chopped
- 6-8 ounce of Acini de Pepe or other tiny pasta, cooked
- 1 small onion, grated
- ⅓ cup fresh Italian parsley, chopped
- 1 large egg
- 2 tablespoons Parmesan cheese, optional
- Salt & pepper

Directions
For meatballs:
- In large bowl, blend first 6 ingredients, toss. Shape into small balls, place on baking sheet.

For soup:
- Bring broth, frozen spinach to boil in large pot. Add uncooked meatballs, simmer a few minutes, stirring occasionally ensuring they don't stick. Add pasta, continue cooking on low boil until pasta, meatballs are cooked about 20 minutes.

Serve
- Season with salt & pepper, sprinkle with Parmesan cheese.

Entree
Prime Rib Roast

Ingredients
- 4 pounds prime rib roast
- ¼ cup butter, softened
- 1 tablespoon fresh ground pepper
- 1 tablespoon herbes de Provence
- Kosher salt

Directions
- Preheat oven to 500°F.
- Place rib roast on plate, bring to room temperature.
- In small bowl, combine butter, pepper, herbes de

Provence. Mix until well blended, spread evenly over entire roast. Season generously with kosher salt.
- Roast prime rib (see Helpful Hint if using a larger or smaller roast) in preheated oven for 20 minutes. Turn oven off leaving roast in oven, door closed for 2 hours. Remove from oven, slice, serve.

Helpful Hints
- Your cooking times vary depending on size of prime rib roast. To calculate your cooking time, multiply exact weight of roast by 5, rounding to the nearest whole number. Cook at 500°F for exactly that many minutes. Example, 6 pound roast: 6x5=30, cooking time is 30 minutes. Turn oven off, wait 2 hours before opening oven.

Side Dish
Mashed Potatoes

Ingredients
- 8-10 medium russet potatoes, about 3 pounds, peeled, cut into quarters
- 1 teaspoon salt
- 2 tablespoons butter
- ¼ cup milk
- Salt & pepper, to taste

Directions
- Place potatoes in large saucepan adding enough water to cover an inch. Bring to boil, reduce heat to medium, cover loosely, boil gently 15–20 minutes until soft, drain well.
- Add milk, butter, salt & pepper, mash until smooth, adding more milk if necessary.

Serve
Place in serving dish with small pat of butter on top.

Side Dish
Buttered Baby Carrots

Ingredients
- 1 package baby carrots
- ¼ teaspoon salt
- ⅛ teaspoon pepper
- ¼ tsp dill, dried or fresh
- ¼ cup butter

Directions
- Place carrots in saucepan, cover with water. Boil for 7-8 minutes until tender, drain water. Add salt, pepper, butter, dill. Toss.

Dessert
Cheese Plate

Ingredients
- 1 baguette, cut into slices
- Assorted cheese; brie, blue, cheddar
- Grapes; green, red

Directions
- Arrange cheeses on large wood cutting board. Place grapes between cheeses.

Serve

Place cutting board with cheese knives on table. Bread in serving basket.

Susannah

by Carlisle Floyd

An opera in two acts by the American composer Carlisle Floyd.
Libretto and music composed while a member of the piano faculty
at Florida State University, awarded Honorary Doctorate of
Humane Letters. Premiered 24 February, 1955.

Floyd adapted the story from the Apocryphal tale of Susannah and the Elders though the latter story has a more positive ending. The story focuses on 18-year-old Susannah Polk, an innocent girl who is targeted as a sinner in the small mountain town of New Hope Valley in the Southern American state of Tennessee.

The opera was awarded the New York Music Critics Circle Award for Best New Opera in 1956 and was chosen to represent American music and culture at the World's Fair at Brussels in 1958. The production was by Frank Corsaro and featured Phyllis Curtin and Norman Treigle. It received its Metropolitan Opera premiere in 1999 with Renée Fleming singing the title role, Jerry Hadley singing Sam and Samuel Ramey singing Blitch. Ramey also recorded the complete opera with Cheryl Studer as Susannah and Jerry Hadley as Sam.

Other well-known sopranos who have portrayed the heroine have included Lee Venora, Joy Clements, Maralin Niska, Nancy Shade, Diana Soviero, Karan Armstrong, Kelly Kaduce and Phyllis Treigle, opposite Michael Devlin as Blitch.

Susannah is one of the most performed American operas, second to Porgy and Bess, and celebrated its 50th anniversary with a performance on the very stage where it premiered at Ruby Diamond Auditorium at Florida State University.

It has been speculated that the opera was inspired by McCarthyism a period of intense fear of communism in America during the early 1950s. The opera also contains many feminist themes that had not been widely explored in popular culture at the time of the opera's writing. Floyd has claimed that this opera, like his other operas, was meant to be different from a traditional opera.

The music is largely characterized by Appalachian folk melodies, some Protestant hymns and some traditional classical music. A particularly prominent part of the opera is Susannah's soaring and melancholy aria in Act II, "The Trees on the Mountain", which is similar to Appalachian folk tunes but is in fact Floyd's own composition.

Appetizer
Mustard Greens with Cornbread

Ingredients
- Mustard greens, 1 pound per person
- Ham hock
- ¼ teaspoon nutmeg
- ½ small onion, diced, optional
- Salt & pepper, to taste

Directions
- Remove tough stems from greens, discard. Wash in cold water.
- Place greens in dutch oven, add 3 inches of water. Add ham hock, nutmeg. Cook on medium heat until tender, 30-45 minutes. Salt & pepper to taste.

Serve
Add onion over greens at table.

Southern Cornbread

Directions

- 2 tablespoons canola oil
- 2 cups yellow cornmeal
- 1 teaspoon salt
- ½ teaspoon baking powder
- ½ teaspoon baking soda
- 1¾ cups fat free buttermilk
- ¼ teaspoon black pepper
- 1 large egg, lightly beaten

Directions

- Preheat oven to 450°F.
- Pour oil into 9-inch cast-iron skillet. Place skillet in oven for 10 minutes.
- In large bowl, combine cornmeal, salt, baking powder, baking soda.
- In medium bowl whisk buttermilk, pepper, egg. Add egg mixture to cornmeal mixture, stirring to moist.
- Remove skillet from oven. Tip pan to coat bottom, sides with oil. Pour excess oil into batter, stir to combine. Pour batter into skillet, spreading evenly. Bake 15 minutes or until a wooden pick inserted into center comes out clean. Let stand 5 minutes before serving.

Entrée

Classic Southern Fried Chicken

Ingredients

- 3½ pounds chicken, cut into 8 or 10 pieces, white, dark, mixed pieces
- ½ teaspoon garlic powder
- 4 eggs
- ½ cup milk
- 2 cups self-rising flour

- Canola oil, for frying
- 1 tablespoon kosher salt
- Fresh black pepper

Directions

- In large bowl, add chicken, salt, add enough water to cover. Cover with plastic wrap, refrigerate 6 hours or overnight to brine.
- Drain chicken, pat dry with paper towels.
- Set up dipping station; one medium sized bowl for egg and milk mixture, a second medium sized bowl for flour, large plate or platter to hold the breaded chicken.
- In medium bowl, whip egg, milk together, dip chicken allowing excess to drip off. Then coat chicken with flour, gently shake off excess, transfer to large platter. Set aside.
- Fill 12 inch or larger cast iron skillet halfway with canola oil. With deep fryer thermometer, heat oil over medium high heat to 360°F degrees. Very carefully slide pieces of chicken in, one at a time, skin side down, slowly laying on hot oil.
- Cook first side about 8 minutes, keep oil at 300°F by adjusting heat up or down. Turn, cook another 6 minutes or until golden brown and juices run clear when pierced with fork. Drain on paper bag or paper towels. Hold the first batch in a low oven while you finish the next batch. Serve immediately.

Helpful Hints

Brining is optional although recommend. It improves flavor, adds moisture, helps to tenderize and can prevent overcooking. If you don't have a thermometer, oil is ready when a pinch of flour sizzles. Be careful oil does not overflow as you add pieces. Don't overcrowd pan, fry 4 or 5 pieces of chicken at a time.

Side Dish
Succotash

Ingredients

- 3 cups water
- 2 cups fresh or frozen baby lima beans
- 1½ cups corn, cut from the cob, 2 average ears
- Salt pork
- Small onion, chopped
- 1 clove garlic, chopped
- 2 tablespoons of butter, melted
- Hot pepper sauce, optional
- Kosher salt, freshly cracked black pepper, to taste

Directions

- In large saucepan, add water, salt pork, onion, garlic.
- Bring water to boil, add beans, return to boil. Reduce heat to medium, cover, cook 25 minutes for fresh, 10 minutes for frozen.
- Add corn, continue cooking for another 5 minutes or until fork tender.
- Drain, toss with butter, season with salt & pepper.

Serve

Serve with hot pepper sauce.

Helpful Hints

For a creamy version, drain, save cooking water. Return beans, corn to pot, add ½ cup heavy cream, enough cooking water to completely cover beans. Cover, simmer for additional 10 to 15 minutes. Add bacon for extra flavor.

Dessert
Skillet Peaches

Ingredients

- 1 pound frozen peaches, sliced, thawed or 4 fresh peaches, peeled, pitted, sliced

- 2 tablespoons fresh lemon juice
- ½ cup unsalted butter
- ¾ cup light brown sugar, packed
- 1 teaspoon cinnamon
- 2 teaspoons pure vanilla extract
- ¼ cup bourbon or whisky, optional
- Pinch salt

Instructions

- If using fresh peaches, toss with lemon juice. If using frozen, omit lemon, set aside.
- In skillet, melt butter, add brown sugar, cinnamon, salt, vanilla, bring to boil. Add bourbon, peaches, cook, stirring regularly until well glazed.

Serve

Over pound cake or ice cream.

Helpful Hint

May also use juice or water in place of bourbon.

Tosca

by Giacomo Puccini

Melodramma in three acts. 1899. Libretto by Giuseppe Giacosa and Luigi Illica after the play La Tosca by Victorien Sardou. First performance at the Teatro Costanzi, Rome, on 14th January 1900.

In the church of Sant' Andrea della Valle, the fugitive Angelotti takes refuge in a private chapel. The painter Cavaradossi returns to the canvas he is painting, a picture of Mary Magdalene influenced by the features of his beloved Tosca and by a woman he has often seen in the church. The sacristan complains of the trouble Cavaradossi gives him.

As he leaves Angelotti emerges from hiding explaining that he has escaped from imprisonment in the Castel Sant'Angelo. The voice of Tosca is heard and Angelotti hides again. Tosca is jealous of what she thinks may have been an assignation with another woman but agrees to meet her lover after her evening performance.

The church fills for a celebration of a supposed victory over Napoleon and Baron Scarpia and his agents seek for signs of Angelotti. Suspicion falls on Cavaradossi as a possible accomplice. Scarpia succeeds now in arousing further jealousy in Tosca who has returned, showing her a fan found in the chapel belonging to Angelotti's sister.

Scarpia orders his men to follow Tosca. When she leaves, a victory Te Deum is sung. In Scarpia's apartment the sound is heard of entertainment being given below for Queen Caroline, dancing and a performance by Tosca. Cavaradossi is arrested, interrogated and when Tosca comes in he is being tortured in the next room to elicit information from her.

She betrays Angelotti's hiding-place at the well in the garden of Cavaradossi's villa. The painter is to be shot at dawn but can be saved if Tosca will give in to Scarpia's demands on her. She pretends to agree and when he has signed a safe-conduct she kills him.

In the third act at Castel Sant'Angelo, Cavaradossi prepares for death as dawn draws near. Tosca is brought in and left alone with him as she explains how there is to be a mock-execution after which they can escape together. In the event Scarpia has his revenge, his orders did not countermand the execution and Cavaradossi is shot. When Tosca realizes that he is dead she leaps from the battlements to her own death while Scarpia's men draw threateningly near having discovered their master's body.

Tosca remains a major work in operatic repertoire although subject to relentlessly hostile criticism on the grounds of the brutal coarseness of its plot. It is, in fact, dramatically convincing up to the moment of final irony. Cavaradossi is entrusted with his first moving aria in the opening act, Recondita armonia (Secret harmony) when he contrasts the dark-haired beauty of Tosca with the fair-haired stranger he has seen in the church both combined in his painting.

Cavaradossi's other great aria comes in the third act as he prepares for death. In E lucevan le stelle (And the stars shone) he regrets his coming execution and parting from Tosca. The role of Tosca has a strong dramatic appeal. Her best-known aria is Vissi d'arte (I have lived for art) as she despairs at the predicament that Scarpia has posed for her.

Appetizer
Arugula with Brûléed Figs, Ricotta, Prosciutto & Smoked Marzipan

Ingredients
- 10 cups baby arugula

For smoked marzipan:
- 1 cup smoked Marcona or smoked regular almonds
- 3 tablespoons grapeseed oil
- 2 tablespoons confectioners' sugar
- 1 teaspoon kosher salt

For crispy prosciutto:
- ½ cup canola oil
- 6 ounces prosciutto, thinly sliced, trimmed of excess fat

For ricotta cream:
- ¾ cup heavy cream, well chilled
- 1 cup, 8 ounces, fresh ricotta
- ¼ teaspoon kosher salt

For brûléed figs:
- 16 fresh figs
- ½ cup turbinado sugar
- 1 tablespoon fleur de sel or flaky sea salts

For dressing:
- ½ cup extra-virgin olive oil
- 1 lemon, juiced

Directions
For smoked marzipan:
- Preheat oven to 350°F, center rack in oven. Line large baking sheet with parchment paper.
- In medium bowl, combine almonds, grapeseed oil, confectioners' sugar, salt, stir to combine. Spread mixture on prepared baking sheet, bake until golden brown, aromatic, 12 to 15 minutes. Transfer to cutting board to cool then coarsely chop.

- **DO AHEAD:** Can be made in advance and stored, in an airtight container at room temperature, up to 5 days.

Fry the prosciutto:
- Line large plate with paper towels.
- In large heavy skillet over moderately high heat, heat oil until shimmering. Working in batches, fry prosciutto, flipping occasionally until golden brown and crispy, about 30 seconds per side. Transfer to paper-towel-lined plate.
- **DO AHEAD**: The prosciutto can be made in advance and stored, in an airtight container at room temperature, up to 4 hours.

Directions for ricotta cream:
- In medium bowl, beat heavy cream until soft peaks form.
- In second medium bowl, combine ricotta, salt, whipping in ½ whipped cream to lighten it. Gently fold the remaining whipped cream until fully incorporated.
- **DO AHEAD:** The ricotta cream can be made in advance and refrigerated, covered, up to 1 hour.

Directions for brûléed figs:
- Preheat broiler, line baking sheet with aluminum foil.
- Trim tops off each fig, cut in half lengthwise. Gently open each fig half, place skin-side-down on baking sheet. Sprinkle with sugar, broil about 6 inches from flame until sugar bubbles, about 90 seconds. Just before serving, sprinkle with fleur de sel.

Directions for dressing:
- In small bowl whisk together olive oil, lemon juice.

Helpful Hint

If Ricotta is too wet, drain before using. Line colander with double layer of cheesecloth, set over small bowl, place ricotta inside, cover with plastic wrap, refrigerate overnight.

Light brown sugar, or raw sugar can be substituted for turbinado.

Serve

Arrange arugula on large serving bowl or platter, drizzle with dressing, toss to coat. Season with salt & pepper, top with smoked marzipan, crispy prosciutto, dollops of ricotta cream, brûléed figs. Serve immediately.

Entrée
Baked Whole Fish with Truffles

Ingredients
- 1½-2 pounds fresh whole fish, such as snapper
- 2 cloves garlic, crushed, minced
- Black truffles, fresh, sliced, approx. 24 slices
- 2 fennel bulb fronds, fresh
- 1 onion, peeled, thinly sliced
- 2 tablespoons truffle oil, divided
- ¼ cup fish stock
- ¼ cup red wine
- 1 cup shiitake or porcini mushrooms, fresh
- Salt & pepper, freshly ground

Directions
- Preheat oven to 400°F.
- Slice fish, sprinkle inside with salt & pepper. Fill cavity with 1 tablespoon garlic, ½ fennel fronds, 5-6 truffle slices per fish. Set aside.
- Line Dutch oven, with tight-fitting lid, with rest of fennel fronds, top with onions. Place the pan over medium heat until fennel smells aromatic.
- Place stuffed fish on top of fennel fronds, onions, pour in fish stock, red wine, drizzle with 1 tablespoon truffle oil. Bring liquids to a boil, scatter mushrooms on top, cover.

- Braise in oven for 25 to 30 minutes.
- Uncover, sprinkle with freshly ground salt & pepper. Place remaining truffle slices, 5-6 per fish, on top, drizzle with remaining truffle oil, cover. Let truffles steam with residual heat 1 to 2 minutes. Serve immediately.

Dessert

Tosca Cake

Ingredients

For cake layer:
- 1¼ cups all-purpose flour
- 1 teaspoon baking powder
- ½ teaspoon coarse salt
- 1 stick butter, melted, cooled
- 1 teaspoon vanilla extract
- ⅓ cup milk
- 3 large eggs
- ¾ cup sugar

For Tosca topping:
- ½ stick butter, melted, cooled
- ⅔ cup sugar
- ¼ cup whipping cream
- 2 tablespoons all-purpose flour
- 1 cup almonds, sliced, flaked
- ¼ teaspoon almond extract
- ¼ teaspoon vanilla extract
- Pinch salt

Directions
- Preheat oven to 350°F.
- Butter, flour 9-inch springform pan. Line bottom of pan with circle of parchment, butter also.
- In small bowl sift flour, baking powder, salt, set aside.
- In medium bowl, mix butter, vanilla, milk, set aside.

- With electric mixer, beat eggs, sugar on high until pale, thick. Alternate adding flour mixture, milk mixture in turns, mixing lightly, ending with dry ingredients. Do not overmix. Pour into prepared pan, bake 20 to 25 minutes until top is barely set.
- While cake is baking, prepare topping. In medium saucepan, combine butter, sugar, cream, flour, salt, over medium-high, stir to combine as butter melts. When combined, add almonds. Let simmer 1 minute, turn off heat, stir in extracts, set aside.
- When cake has baked for 20 to 25 minutes and just barely set, gently remove from oven, raise oven temperature to 400°F.
- Gently spread topping on cake. Place cake back in the oven, bake additional 15 minutes or so until topping is golden brown. Cool before slicing.

Historical Opera Dishes from the Artists

Giacomo Casanova

Venice 1725–1798

Life & History

Giacomo Casanova was orphaned by his father, Gaetano Farussi, although some believe his biological father was a nobleman named Michele Grimaldi. His mother, Zanetta Farussi, was an actress and left young Giacomo in the care of his grandmother.

Giacomo was originally educated by a tutor but then entered seminar school with the intention of joining the clergy. He received minor duties but eventually was kicked out for his forbidden love affairs. He was, however, a brilliant intellectual. He was a literary, alchemist, musician and politician but above all a great storyteller and lover of women.

Some people believed he was a spy for the Venetian Doges, perhaps due to his countless trips throughout Europe and his friendship with many kings and nobles who both trusted and admired him. His worldliness however did not keep him out of prison. He was imprisoned for turning against the state and placed in "the Leads," the famous prison attached to the Doge's palace. He was able to escape and fled to France where he changed his name buying himself the noble title of Chevalier de Seingalt.

He made money as an occultist, convincing various aristocrats he could heal them with supernatural powers. He ended his career as a librarian to Count Waldstein.

Casanova owes his lasting fame to his memoirs, in which he documents his libertine lifestyle, love affairs and general depiction of life at the time.

Casanova's Sucking Veal Liver

This recipe comes from the L'Apicio moderno, a recipe book written by Francesco Leonardi in 1790. Casanova was aware of the sublime art of using food and recipes for seduction and this dish, typical of his city is not a lessening example of Casanova's image.

Ingredients
- 1 pound calf liver, finely sliced
- 1 pound of onions, thinly sliced
- 1 ¾ oz extra virgin olive oil
- 1 ounce butter
- White wine, to taste
- Meat broth, to taste
- Polenta
- Salt & ground black pepper

Directions
- In casserole dish gently simmer oil, butter, onions, drop of broth.
- Add liver, sprinkle with wine, cook at high heat, salt & pepper to taste.

Helpful Hint
In Leonardi's recipe, once cooked, a handful of chopped parsley was added along with a few tablespoons of gravy and lots of lemon juice.

Serve
Accompany liver with polenta.

Enrico Caruso
Naples 1873-1921

Life & History

Enrico Caruso was born into a poor Neapolitan family. Enrico was sent to school until he was ten at which point he went to work with his father in the foundry. His mother wanted him to continue studying and enrolled him in night school. He discovered that he was both a gifted artist and singer.

Enrico first began to sing in the church choir and began to hold concerts with other passionate singers in local coffee shops as a way to add to the family income. He met Eduardo Missino who introduced Enrico to his first opera teacher Guglielmo Vergine. During this time he had been called to report for military service but his brother was sent instead so that Enrico could continue his studies. He made his debut in 1894 in L'amico Francesco by Domenico Morelli beginning his career as a professional singer.

After touring Europe, Argentina and Russia, Enrico sang at La Scala and was directed by Toscanini. Enrico's voice and vocal capabilities were criticized, however, after a performance at San Carlo, the opera theater in his own hometown of Naples. After receiving the criticism Enrico swore never to return to San Carlo. Instead, he was invited to perform in London, Munich and at the Metropolitan Opera House in New York. Enrico was a loved performer and was considered the greatest tenor of all times. He can also be credited as the first opera singer to make a record.

Enrico Caruso's Naples Style Bucatini

This recipe was created by the great tenor who loved more than everything else the pasta typical of his native Naples. The story has it that since he was given a cold reception by his fellow-citizens, Caruso swore he would never sing in Naples again but he would return there only to enjoy his favorite macaroni.

Ingredients
- ⅝ pound bucatini
- 3-4 San Marzano tomatoes, chopped
- 1 bell pepper, cut in chunks
- 1 zucchini, cut in rounds
- 1 garlic clove, cut in quarters
- 1 chili pepper, crushed
- Extra virgin olive oil
- Oregano, basil, parsley, chopped

Directions
- In large skillet, saute garlic cloves in oil, remove when golden. Add tomatoes, pepper, turn up heat. Add oregano, chili pepper, generous amount of basil, simmer on medium heat.
- Coat zucchini with flour, deep-fry in medium pain with 2 inches oil.
- Cook pasta al dente in salted boiling water, drain.

Serve
Top pasta with tomato sauce, add deep-fried zucchini, sprinkle with chopped parsley.

Giuseppe Verdi
Parma, Milan 1813 -1901

Life and History

Born into a poor family Giuseppe showed early signs of his brilliant mind and musical talent. His father placed him under the care of the state so that he would receive an elementary education. First his priest, then the organist recognized Giuseppe's gift and encouraged him to study music in order to one day become a great organist.

Giuseppe's talent attracted the attention of a businessman, Antonio Barezzi, who generously supported Verdi's career, encouraging him to attend a real music school. Verdi married Margherita, the Barezzi's daughter, while applying for acceptance into the conservatory in Milan. He was rejected because "he wasn't talented enough" musically. Verdi continued to study privately with Vincenzo Lavigna. Under Lavigna he wrote his first opera called Oberto.

Verdi achieved his first big success thanks to the opera impresario Merelli who gave the musician the libretto for Nabucco. With his musis he became a beacon of hope for national unity supporting the independence movement both artistically and financially.

In the years to come, Verdi dedicated himself to making more refined, mature music. He reached the apex of his artistic career with his later operas.

He died far from home in Milan, where he was given a glorious funeral and laid to rest among the greats.

Risotto Giuseppe Verdi Style

This dish was created by the French chef Henry-Paul Pellaprat (1869-1952) and dedicated to the Maestro.

Ingredients
- ¾ pounds Carnaroli rice
- 2 ounces butter
- 3 ounces mushrooms, thinly sliced
- 3 ounce asparagus tips
- 3 ounce Prosciutto di Parma, finely minced
- 3 ounce canned tomatoes, peeled, seeded, cubed
- 3½ tablespoon light cream
- 3 cup meat broth
- ½ onion, minced
- Parmigiano-Reggiano cheese, grated

Directions
- In large pot, melt ¼ portion butter, add onion slowly cook until soft and golden.
- Add rice, toast for 1 minute. Add stock, 1 ladle at a time, waiting until stock has been absorbed before adding the next, cook over medium heat for 8-10 minutes.
- Add mushrooms, prosciutto, asparagus and tomatoes. Stir well, cook for 2 minutes, add cream. When al dente, about 18 minutes, add butter, Parmigiano-Reggiano cheese, stir well and cover with lid.

Helpful Hint
Let rest for 2 minutes, serve.

Giuseppe Verdi considered himself a country boy of Bassa. He loved the land and the fruits of his homeland. He used to take them with him on his trips or have them sent to him. One of his favorite products from Bassa was cooked pork shoulder. He often gave a shoulder as a gift to his closest friends, with the instructions for how to use it:

"Before cooking the shoulder ham, reduce the salt content by soaking it in warm water for two hours. After that, place the shoulder ham into a pot, large enough for it and fill the pot with water; bring it to the boil and cook over a gentle heat for at least six hours. Leave to cool in its own cooking liquid, then take the shoulder ham out of the pot, dry it and it is ready to serve."..Giuseppe Verdi. The Maestro particularly liked this dish when still hot.

Gioacchino Rossini
Pesaro–Paris 1792-1868

Life & History

Gioacchino Rossini was born into a family of musicians. His father a horn player and his mother an opera singer. He moved with them to Bologna where he too began working as a musician.

He enrolled in a musical conservatory and attended classes taught by Father Mattei. It was here that he wrote his first opera Demetrio e Polibio. After he finished school he dedicated himself completely to music.

In 1813 after having composed his first successful opera, Tandcredi, he was asked to write additional operas for Barbaia, a local theater impresario.

Rossini composed a long series for Barbaia, including Il barbiere di Siviglia ("The Barber of Seville"), La gazza ladra ("The Thieving Magpie"), and Semiramide ("Semiramis").

In 1823 he moved to Paris where he became the director of the Italian theater and Inspector General to the King. In Paris he wrote his masterpiece, "William Tell", performed in 1829. Rossini moved back to Italy for about twenty years eventually returning to his home in Paris for the last years of his life.

King of the 19th century musical scene, Rossini was also a famous food lover. Not only did he come from a region where food was the center of life, but he went to school in Bologna, also known as La Grassa or "The Fat One" and then moved to Paris. His life revolved around the most famous food cities in Europe.

Rossini's Tournedos

His modest upbringing caused him to really appreciate the pleasures of fine food. He particularly loved truffles and foie gras. Recipes are still being attributed to him today, and he inspired many others during the course of his career.

Ingredients
- Beef fillet
- 1 stick butter
- 6 slices fois gras
- 6 slices black truffle
- 6 slices bread
- 1 tablespoon Madera wine
- String

Directions
- Tie fillet slices with string to retain their round shape while cooking

- In large saute pan, brown fillet in butter until medium-rare, remove from pan, remove string when cooked.
- Spread butter on bread, gently fry in oil remove to plate, keep warm.
- Pour Madera wine into meat juices and reduce.

Serve
- Arrange tournedos on each bread slice, top with slice of foie gras, garnish with truffle shavings (saute in butter for extra flavor). Pour Madera wine reduction over tournedos to serve.

Antonio de Curtis (Toto)
Naples 1898-1967

Life & History

When De Curtis died suddenly at the age of 69 it was said that with him went the last character in the Italian tradition of Commedia dell'arte.

Antonio was born from an illicit relationship between his mother Anna Clemente and Giuseppe de Curtis. He was raised in Rione Sanità one of the most popular and populated areas of Naples. Antonio remained tied to his city and many of his characters were truly Neapolitan in their interest in food and love and their personalities ranged from witty to simply mad.

Antonio's mother had hopes that he would become a priest but Antonio had already begun acting in small local theaters by the age of fifteen. He performed with other young actors including De Filippo. In the poor, improvised theaters De Curtis memorized scenes without a script giving his unique physicality to the characters. He was known for his floppy puppet movements, expressive face and comedic phrases that have entered into day-to-day speech.

His acting reached new levels in Rome, appearing in his first film in 1937. He then returned to the theater with new energy and new acting partners, Anna Magnani and the De Filippo brothers. His artistic career blossomed from 1947 to 1952 in both the theater and on the big screen. During the years to come he experimented with different avenues including television.

Spaghetti alla Gennaro

This recipe comes from a cookbook De Curtis daughter, Liliana, dedicated to him. It is a simple dish of the common folk and captures the Neapolitan spirit that Totò portrayed many times on the big screen and theater stages.

Ingredients
- 1 pound spaghetti
- 3 slices stale bread
- 4 salted anchovies, chopped
- Basil
- Oregano, garlic, basil
- Extra virgin olive oil

Directions
- Rub bread slices with garlic, arrange on plate.
- In large saute pan, saute two garlic cloves in two tablespoons of oil, do not let garlic brown. Toss in bread until crispy, remove to plate.
- In large saucepan, cook spaghetti al dente, drain.
- To saute pan, add two tablespoons oil, anchovies, pinch of oregano.
- Add pasta to pan. Add crispy bread, stir quickly, add handful of basil leaves, torn into pieces.

Catherine de' Medici

Firenze-Blois 1519-1589

Life & History

The great granddaughter of Lorenzo il Magnifico and wife of Henry II of France, Catherine was one of the most important women of the Renaissance. Remembered for her great ability to manage the kingdom during its religious battles and plots against the palace, France remained a united nation allowing her to pass on the throne to her children.

Catherine was married for political reasons at 14. Her arrival in France was a major disappointment expecting her handsome French husband to marry an attractive, well-bred girl, not a foreigner from a common family. To make matters worse Catherine was not able to conceive for almost 10 years.

The queen did not lose hope and accepted all medical advice given to her by the Court's doctors. Some believe her eventual conception may have been due to the doctors advice she received regarding her diet. She brought a handful of reliable chefs with her when she moved encouraging them to serve the royal couple a special diet to improve fertility. Catherine eventually had nine children.

Bringing with her many Tuscan customs to France, she decorated her tables elegantly with flowers, sugar sculptures and forks which had long been used in Florence but were almost never found on French tables. She introduced olive oil, Chianti wines and white beans to the French culinary lexicon and suggested that savory and sweet flavors be separated.

Tuscan Cibreo

Cibreo is a typical Florentine recipe that is closely connected to a French dish called finanzière which comes from the Piemontese recipe for finanziera.

Ingredients
- 1 pound chicken livers, gently chopped
- 1 onion, chopped
- 4 leaves sage
- 1¾ ounce butter
- 2 tablespoons Extra virgin olive oil
- 2 egg yolks
- ½ lemon
- Broth
- All-purpose flour
- Salt & ground black pepper

Directions
- In large saute pan, gently fry onion in oil, butter without letting it brown.
- Add chicken livers, beans, onion, two leaves of sage, season with salt & pepper
- Cook on moderate heat for 10 minutes, moistening with a few drops of broth.
- In small bowl, beat egg yolks, lemon juice.
- Remove pot from heat, add egg mixture.

Serve
Allow to rest for a few minutes, serve on slices of lightly toasted Tuscan bread.

Opera Singers Favorites

Alfredo Sauce & Fettucine
by Wayne Line

One of Violetta Zabi's favorites.

Ingredients
- ¼ cup butter
- 5-10 garlic cloves crushed
- 1 quart heavy cream
- ¼ teaspoon nutmeg
- 1 cup grated Parmesan cheese
- Salt & fresh ground pepper, to taste

Directions
- In medium saucepan, melt butter over medium heat until melted. Add garlic, cook 2-3 minutes until it starts to brown. Add cream, bring to a boil allowing cream to start to thicken, 10-15 minutes. Add nutmeg, cheese, salt & pepper.
- Heat 5-10 minutes until cheese is incorporated and melted. Pour over cooked fettucine.

Helpful Hint
Sauce will thicken when added to noodles.
Any noodles can be used.

Serve
Toss to coat noodles, serve in pasta dish.
Sprinkle extra Parmesan on top when serving.

Classic Bread Pudding with Vanilla Sauce
by Jacqueline Ornsby
Soprano, Nickel City Opera, Co-president & Host of OperaBuffs WNY Inside Opera Lecture Series

Directions
- 4 cups white bread, cubed, about 8 slices
- ½ cup raisins, optional

- 2 cups milk
- ¼ cup butter
- ½ cup sugar
- 2 eggs, slightly beaten
- 1 tablespoon vanilla
- ½ teaspoon ground nutmeg

For sauce:
- ½ cup butter
- ½ cup sugar
- ½ cup brown sugar, firmly packed
- ½ cup heavy whipping cream
- 1 tablespoon vanilla

Directions
For pudding:
- Heat oven to 350°F. Grease 1½ quart casserole with butter.
- In large bowl, combine bread, raisins.
- In medium saucepan, combine milk, butter, cook over medium heat until butter is melted, about 4 to 7 minutes. Pour milk mixture over bread; let stand 10 minutes.
- Stir in remaining pudding ingredients.
- Bake 40-50 minutes or until set in center.

Directions
For sauce:
- In 1-quart saucepan, combine all sauce ingredients except vanilla. Cook over medium heat, stirring occasionally until mixture thickens, comes to a full boil, about 5 to 8 minutes. Stir in vanilla.

Serve
Spoon warm pudding into individual dessert dishes, pour over sauce. Store leftovers in refrigerator.

Friûlan Polenta
Soft Polenta with Sautéed Mushrooms, Arugula,
Fried Egg & Black Truffle Essence
by Suzanne Fatta

This is a recipe from the Friuli-Venezia-Guilia region of Italy, just north of Venice where I lived and visited while singing Baroque operas in the city. Friuli is the home of polenta and they're even called "Polentone' by Southerners.

Ingredients
- 1 cup stone ground polenta, I prefer yellow
- 1 cup dry or semi-sec white wine, preferably a Collio, Colli Orientalist or Tocai from Friuli
- 3 cups water or vegetable stock
- ½ cup grated Parmigiano cheese
- Assortment of mushrooms, gently cleaned, sliced
- Shallots, diced
- Thyme, fresh
- Extra virgin olive oil
- 1 or 2 eggs, per portion
- Olive oil
- Arugula, large fresh bag
- Salt & pepper to taste

Directions
- In tall, heavy pasta pot, heat water or stock, wine until boiling, reduce heat add polenta in slow, consistent stream with one hand, whisking with the other. Stir until smooth, add salt & pepper to taste.
- In the meantime, in sauté pan, in Extra virgin olive oil sauté shallots, sprinkle of salt until soft, transparent.
- Add mushrooms, ground black pepper, thyme. Continue to cook mushrooms until caramelized and most of liquid is cooked off. Deglaze with a bit of wine.

- Keep stirring polenta, add grated cheese at the end.
- Once polenta and mushrooms are done, set aside off heat.
- Fry 1-2 eggs per portion in Extra virgin olive oil, salt & pepper, fried to your preference but I like it when soft yoke brakes and forms a sauce in the bowl.
- Ladle polenta into bowls, layer mushrooms, fried eggs on top. Add arugula, top with truffle essence, fresh grind of pepper.

Helpful Hint

Truffle oil is ok but it's really better with black truffle paste.

Pasta E Fagioli Al Tenore
Tenor's Pasta & Beans
by Salvatore Licretia, Salvatores
Italian Restaurant, Buffalo, NY

Ingredients
- 1 pound sweet Italian sausage
- ¼ pound bacon or pancetta, chopped
- 1 pound ground beef
- 1 onion, finely chopped
- 2 celery stalks, diced
- 2 garlic cloves, chopped fine
- 4 cups chicken or turkey stock
- 1 8 ounce can tomato sauce
- 2 19 ounce cans cannellini beans, drained, divided
- 1 15 ounce can red kidney beans, drained
- 1 14 ounce can tomatoes, drained, seeded, chopped
- 1½ cups (12 ounces) ditalini or other tubular pasta
- 1 cup orzo, cooked
- 1 carrot, sliced
- ½ teaspoon white pepper
- 1 teaspoon thyme
- 1 teaspoon rosemary

- 1 teaspoon basil
- Parmigiano, shredded, grated as garnish
- Basil, chopped as garnish

Directions

- In large, heavy pot cook sausage in small amount of water until browned about 10 minutes. Remove sausages to plate, cool, chop into pieces, finely grind in food processor.
- Brown bacon or pancetta in same pot, add a touch of olive oil to prevent burning if necessary.
- When browned, not crisp, add chopped sausage, ground beef, cook until brown about 15 minutes.
- Add onions, celery, garlic, cook 5 minutes, stirring constantly. Add stock, skim top to remove excess fat. Simmer 10 to 15 minutes.
- In food processor, blend tomato sauce, 1 cup cannellini beans until smooth. Pour mixture into pot, add remaining cannellini beans, kidney beans, tomatoes, herbs. Simmer 5 minutes, add pasta, simmer for additional 20 minutes.
- Add orzo and carrots, simmer for an additional 10 minutes.

Helpful Hint

- Add more water or stock for a thick stew like consistency.

Serve

Serve with grated Parmigiana cheese, chopped basil.

Puccini Primavera
by Valerian Ruminski
Bass & General Director, Nickel City Opera

Ingredients

- Handful of organic spinach
- Handful of mushrooms

- 2 tablespoons coconut oil
- Heaping tablespoon of minced garlic
- Gluten free spaghetti
- Parmesan cheese

Directions

- In medium pan, saute garlic in coconut oil until brown, add mushrooms, spinach until wilted, set aside.
- Boil large pot of salted water, add spaghetti, cook al dente. Drain.

Serve

Divide pasta evenly on plates, top with spinach and mushroom mixture, generous amount of Parmesan cheese.

Rueben Slaw
from Jacqueline Quirk, Soprano

Ingredients

- Half Head of green cabbage
- 1 pound pastrami or corned beef
- ½ pound of Imported Swiss cheese
- 12 ounces avocado oil mayo
- ½ cup dill pickles
- 2 teaspoons apple cider vinegar
- 1 teaspoon monkfruit sweetener

Directions

- Cut end of cabbage off, cut in half lengthwise, julienne cut into roughly ¼ inch thick strips. Dice dill pickles.
- Cut pastrami or corned beef, Swiss cheese into roughly ¼ inch strips
- In small mixing bowl, add mayo, apple cider vinegar, monkfruit sweetner, dill pickles, mix well.
- In extra large mixing bowl add half cabbage mixture, mix with half of mayo mixture. Add remaining halves, incorporate together. Serve immediately or store in refrigerator up to 2-3 days.

Opera Buffs Obsession

Cream of Chicken Broccoli Soup
by Hedy Kunstman, friend of Delaware Valley Opera

"Folks for whom I've made this go 'mad' about it."

Ingredients
- ½ pound chicken pieces, cubed, cooked
- 4 cups water or chicken broth
- 1 10 ounce can cream of celery soup
- 10 ounce frozen chopped broccoli or 2 crowns, fresh
- ½ cup butter
- 1 large onion, chopped
- ¼ cup flour
- 2 cups milk
- Celery leaves, chives, sage
- 2 teaspoon salt,
- ½ teaspoon pepper
- ¼ cup shredded cheddar cheese, optional
- Water

Directions
- In large pot, simmer chicken in 4 cups water, add celery leaves, chives, sage until soft. Remove chicken, save broth.
- Add celery soup, bring to boil. Add broccoli, bring to second boil, cover, reduce heat, simmer 5 minutes until broccoli is soft.
- In saute pan, melt butter, saute onions for 5 minutes until tender. Add flour, cook 1 minute, stirring to remove lumps. Slowly stir milk into pot with broth and broccoli, add onion mixture. Cook until thickened, stirring constantly.
- Add salt, pepper, chicken stirring frequently.

Serve
- Ladle into bowls, top with shredded cheddar cheese.

Del Posto's Fusilli with Pesto & Peperonata
from Sylvia Volk

Ingredients
For pesto:
- 4 cups basil leaves, packed
- 1 garlic clove, roughly chopped
- ¾ cup olive oil
- ¾ cup grated Parmigiano-Reggiano cheese
- 1 pound fusilli, cooked

Helpful Hint
Try with gluten free pasta. Makes 1 cup.

Ingredients
For Peperonata:
- 3 tablespoons olive oil
- ½ teaspoon red pepper flakes, crushed
- 1 14 ounce can San Marzano tomatoes, crushed
- 1 tablespoon red wine vinegar
- ½ tablespoon sugar
- 1 garlic clove, thinly sliced
- 1 anchovy fillet, roughly chopped
- ½ medium white onion, thinly sliced
- ½ fennel bulb, thinly sliced
- 1 roasted red pepper, deseeded, sliced
- Salt & pepper, to taste

Directions
For Pesto:
- Build an ice bath.
- Boil a pot of salted water. Blanch the basil in boiling water until bright green, soft, about 5 seconds. Remove basil with slotted spoon or fine-mesh sieve, plunge into ice bath to stop cooking. Drain immediately, squeeze basil dry.
- Transfer basil to blender add garlic, olive oil, purée until smooth.

- Transfer to mixing bowl, stir in grated che

Helpful Hint

For ice bath: fill a large bowl with ice, cold water.

Directions

For Peperonata:

- In medium saucepan over medium-high neat, add 1 tablespoon olive oil, red pepper flakes. Allow red pepper flakes to bloom in oil 5 to 10 seconds.
- Add tomatoes, vinegar, sugar, cook stirring often until tomatoes reduce to a jam-like consistency, 12 to 15 minutes. Season with salt, let cool.
- In separate saucepan over medium-high heat, add remaining 2 tablespoons of olive oil. When hot, add garlic, anchovy, cook until anchovy begins to disintegrate and garlic turns light golden brown. Add white onion, fennel, cook until tender 8 to 10 minutes. Remove from heat, toss in roasted red pepper. Allow mixture to cool, roughly chop.
- Combine with tomato paste, season with salt & pepper.

Helpful Hint

Makes 1¾ cups.

Serve

Toss fusilli with pesto. Dollop peperonata on top.

Lasagna
by Margaret Breen, Soprano, Nickel City Opera Volunteer

Ingredients

- 1 large (24 ounce) jar pasta sauce
- 15 ounce whole milk ricotta cheese
- 1 8 ounce mozzarella cheese, sliced
- Parmesan cheese
- 1 8 ounce box lasagna noodles, cooked
- Ground turkey, cooked, browned

- 1 teaspoon nutmeg

Directions

- Preheat oven to 375°F. Prepare a large 9x13 glass baking pan.
- In large bowl, add cooked ground turkey to pasta sauce, set aside.
- In small bowl, stir nutmeg into ricotta cheese.
- Spread a thin coating of meat sauce on bottom on baking pan to prevent sticking. Place enough lasagna noodles, in single layer, to cover bottom of pan.
- Add another layer of meat sauce on top, add layer of mozzarella cheese, ricotta cheese, spreading bottom evenly. Sprinkle with parmesan cheese.
- Add another layer of lasagna noodles, repeat layers. Finish with layer of noodles, meat sauce, sliced mozzarella, sprinkle with parmesan cheese.
- Cover with foil, bake for approximately 30 minutes. Remove foil and continue baking until cheese is melted, another 10-15 minutes.

Serve

Allow to cool for at least 15 minutes before serving. Serve with extra sauce on side.

Sopa de Elote

Ingredients

- 4 cups fresh corn kernels, cut, scraped from 5-6 ears of corn or two 10 ounce packages frozen corn kernels
- 4½ cups milk
- ¼ cup butter, softened
- 1 teaspoon sea salt
- 2 poblano chiles, peeled, seeded, diced
- 6 tablespoons Monterey Jack cheese, shredded
- 6 corn tortillas, cut in thin strips, fried crisp

Helpful Hint

Fresh or frozen corn only, never use canned corn.

Directions

- Combine corn, 1 cup milk in blender, puree at high speed until smooth, set aside.
- In 3-quart stock pot, heat butter over medium heat until melted, bubbly. Add corn puree, cook over medium heat for about 5 minutes, stirring constantly. Add remaining 3½ cups milk, sea salt; bring mixture to boil.
- Reduce heat to low, simmer 15 minutes, stirring to avoid sticking.

Serve

Warm soup bowls in low oven, add 1 tablespoon each diced chiles, shredded cheese. Ladle hot soup into bowls, garnish with a few tortilla strips.

Spinach, Beet & Quinoa Salad
by Colleen Eder, Dietitian Consultant,
Erie County Senior Services

Ingredients

- 1 bunch of spinach
- 1 medium beet
- 2 cups cooked quinoa, cooled
- ¼ cup hazelnuts
- 3 tablespoons grapeseed oil
- 4 tablespoons red wine vinegar
- 1½ tablespoon honey
- ¼ teaspoon salt
- Salt & pepper, to taste

Directions

- Preheat oven to 375°F. Scrub beets, wrap in foil, roast 45 minutes or until soft.
- Chop hazelnuts, spread on baking sheet, roast in oven with beets a few minutes.

- When beets are cooked, remove from oven, let cool. Peel off skins, chop into 1 inch pieces.
- In small bowl combine grapeseed oil, red wine vinegar, honey, sea salt.

Helpful Hint

Add beets at last minute, do not mix in, unless you don't mind eating a pink salad.

Serve

In large serving bowl toss spinach, quinoa, hazelnuts. Add dressing, toss well. Top with beets. Season with salt & pepper.

La Pizza Con Funghi
by Seymour Barab

A spoof of opera for the love of opera. La Pizza con Fungi (Pizza with Mushrooms) is a slapstick farce that parodies Italian opera of the 19th century. Opera has a reputation for being an uber-traditional, high-brow art form featuring larger-than-life characters, tragic love triangles, dramatic deaths and soaring, glorious music.

Seymour Barab's parody of 19th century opera, La Pizza con Funghi, will touch your funny bone! In this homage to a beloved art form, we encounter the characters found in many operas. The soprano, in love with the tenor, plots to poison her older baritone husband. Her mezzo maid, in love with the baritone, spills the beans and as in so many operas, no one is left alive at the final curtain!

It's a fun way to reach out and go out to a different location and put opera in a place you wouldn't normally think of.

La Pizza con Funghi features four roles: Voluptua, the new wife of the exuberant but somewhat clueless Count Formaggio, is attempting to have an affair with debonair tenor

Scorpio and decides to kill the count by feeding him a pizza topped with poisonous mushrooms.

Voluptua's maid, the aptly named Phobia, thwarts the poisoning attempt as the whole plot turns hilariously awry.

While the opera is comedic and the characters are broadly drawn, the focus is still on the music. There are no rules because it's making fun of opera, we don't have to follow any of the rules, we get to make fun of them.

Wild Mushroom Pizza
with Caramelized Onions, Fontina & Rosemary
by Seymour Barab

Ingredients
- 8 tablespoons (½ cup) butter, divided
- 3 tablespoons grapeseed oil
- 3 onions, halved lengthwise, thinly sliced crosswise
- 2 pounds assorted wild mushrooms, crimini, oyster, chanterelle, stemmed shiitake, cut in bite-size pieces
- Garlic cloves, minced
- 1 medium shallot, minced
- 2 cups dry white wine
- 1 tablespoon fresh rosemary, minced
- Italian seasonings, optional
- Cornmeal, for dusting
- Garlic oil
- Salt & pepper
- Pizza Dough, purchased or homemade, recipe below
- 3 cups (10 ounces) grated Fontina cheese

Directions
- Preheat oven to 500°F.
- In large skillet, melt 4 tablespoon butter, 2 tablespoon grapeseed oil on medium heat.

- Add onions, sauté until golden, season with salt & pepper, set aside. Wipe skillet with paper towel.
- Melt remaining 4 tablespoons butter, 1 teaspoon grapeseed oil over medium high heat. Add mushrooms, garlic, shallot, saute 4 minutes.
- Add wine, simmer until almost all liquid is absorbed, stirring frequently about 13 minutes.
- Add rosemary, optional Italian seasonings, season with salt & pepper.
- Position oven rack in bottom third of oven. Place heavy 17x11 inch baking sheet on rack, invert if rimmed.
- Roll out 2 dough disks on lightly floured surface to 8-inch rounds, allowing dough to rest a few minutes if it springs back. Sprinkle another baking sheet, invert if rimmed, with cornmeal.
- Lightly brush dough with garlic oil.
- Sprinkle with ½ cup cheese, scatter 2½ tablespoons onions over cheese, scatter ½ cup mushrooms over onions. Sprinkle with salt.
- Repeat with second dough disk, garlic oil, cheese, onions, mushrooms and salt.
- Transfer dough with paddle or large spatula to hot baking sheet in oven.
- Bake pizzas 6 minutes, rotate pizzas half a turn. Bake until crust is deep brown, about 6 minutes longer.
- Using large spatula, carefully transfer pizzas to cutting board. Let rest 1 minute. Slice into wedges and serve.
- Repeat with remaining ingredients.

For Dough:
- 2 (¼ ounce) packages active dry yeast
- 5½ cups unbleached all-purpose flour, plus additional for dusting
- 2 cups warm water (105–115F), divided

- 2 teaspoons salt
- 1 teaspoon sugar, optional

Directions

- Whisk together yeast, 2 tablespoons flour, ½ cup warm water in measuring cup. Let stand until mixture develops a creamy foam, about 10 minutes. If mixture doesn't foam, discard and start over with new yeast.
- In large bowl, stir together salt, 3 cups flour. Add yeast mixture, remaining 1½ cups warm water, stir until smooth, then stir in 1 cup more flour. If dough sticks to your fingers, stir in just enough flour, up to ¾ cup a little at a time to make dough just come away from side of bowl. Add 1 teaspoon sugar, if using.
- Knead dough on lightly floured surface with floured hands, lightly re-flour work surface, hands when dough becomes too sticky, until dough is smooth, soft, elastic about 10 minutes.
- Divide dough in half, form into 2 balls, generously dust balls with flour, put each in medium bowl. Cover bowls with plastic wrap and let rise in a draft-free place at warm room temperature until doubled, 1 to 1¼ hours.

Helpful Hint

This dough may be wetter than other pizza doughs you have made.

For sweeter dough add 1 teaspoon of sugar.

Serves

Six 8 inch pizzas.

Opera Sweets

by Sylvia Volk

Fudge

History

There are several theories explaining why this fudge is connected to opera, one of them being "the opera is something rich, at the top, like opera fudge."

Opera fudge is one of many delicious culinary specialties connected with Lebanon, PA. This fondant candy is a seasonal treat traditionally made from Thanksgiving to Easter as it melts in the hotter months. In other parts of the country these candies are called opera drops, french creams and opera caramels. Cincinnati's famous Opera Creams are a chocolate-coated fondant.

Opera drops were chocolates with vanilla cream filling, kind of conical, haystack shaped. You could buy them at intermission at the opera. There was a British brand called Between the Acts that you could buy at Bailey's in Boston. There was also a variety of fondant called opera caramels which had cream amongst its ingredients in the late 19th and early 20th centuries.

Chocolate Opera Fudge

Ingredients
- 3 squares bitter chocolate
- 2 cups sugar
- 1 cup cream
- 1 teaspoon corn syrup
- 1 teaspoon orange extract
- Pinch of salt

Directions
- In medium saucepan melt chocolate over low heat. Gradually add rest of ingredients, bring to boil at 230°F, stirring carefully to prevent burning to 238°F or until candy forms a soft ball when dropped in cold water.

- Pour on marble slab, let cool slightly. Knead until creamy, flavor with orange extract, shape into small balls, let harden.

Vanilla Opera Fudge

- 2 cups sugar
- 1 cup heavy cream
- ⅛ teaspoon cream of tartar
- 1 teaspoon vanilla extract

Directions

- In medium saucepan stir sugar, cream over low heat until dissolved. Add cream of tartar, bring to boil stirring carefully to prevent burning to 238°F or until candy forms a soft ball when dropped in cold water.
- Pour on slightly moistened marble slab or large platter allowing to cool. With broad spatula work candy back and forth until creamy. It may take some time, but it will surely change if it was boiled to the right temperature. Cover with damp cloth for ½ hour.
- Add vanilla, blend well. Press into 9x12 square pan lined with wax paper, let stand to harden, cut in squares.

Helpful Hint

Move thermometer often when boiling to prevent candy from burning underneath.

Opera Creams

History

Originating in Cincinnati, the Papas family can be credited with the invention of the opera cream candy. Chris Papas, Sr. was a Greek who immigrated to the United States from Macedonia in 1909. His son, Chris Jr. helped his father support the family by cleaning furnaces and delivering coal from the time he was 11 years old.

They were trying to make a dollar any way that they could when they decided to experiment with candy recipes in the basement of their home. They came up with a candy they liked and began selling it on street corners.

When business was slow in the warm months, they started making ice cream opening an ice cream parlor and soda shop. In 1935, in the midst of the Great Depression, they set up a retail shop named Lily's Candies named after Chris Jr's mother. Chris left school after the eighth grade to help his father make the candy by hand, full-time. In 1942 he met his future wife, Ann Zappa, having asked her to work in the burgeoning candy shop.

He was inducted into the Army and was stationed in West Virginia. During the summer of 1943, Ann traveled to West Virginia to marry him before he was shipped out to Europe to fight in World War II in the Battle of the Bulge. After the war, Chris Jr. returned to Covington and to the growing candy business. He designed machines to make candy in order to keep up with demand. Today Papas opera creams are popular from Washington, D.C., to Arizona. The factory makes as many as 100,000 eggs in an eight-hour day during peak season, the three months before Easter.

Mr. Papas bought the production side of the business and renamed it Chris A. Papas & Son when his father retired in 1957. His sister Katherine Papas Hartmann purchased Lily's Candies and operated it until she sold it to her brother in 1987.

Opera Creams

Ingredients
- ¾ cup milk
- 2 cups sugar
- 2 squares chocolate

Directions
- In medium saucepan, melt milk, sugar, chocolate. Boil 3-4 minutes.
- Set in cool place until cold, then beat until mixture becomes creamy.
- Shape into balls, drop on waxed paper. Chill.

Opera BonBons

As a slight variation, shape Opera Creams in small balls, adding a piece of nut, cherry, or marshmallow in the center of each.

After the Opera Favorites

Almond Chocolate Chip Opera Cookies for a Busy Soprano
by Danielle DiStefano, soprano

"A variation of the revered flavors of the world famous Opera Cake."

Ingredients
- 2¾ cups all purpose flour
- 1 teaspoon baking soda
- 1 cup (2 sticks) butter, softened
- ¾ cup granulated sugar
- ¾ cup light brown sugar, packed
- 2 eggs, large
- 1 teaspoon vanilla extract
- 2-4 teaspoons almond extract
- 2 cups semi-sweet chocolate chips
- 1 teaspoon salt

For Espresso Ganache:
- 1 cup heavy cream
- 1 cup semi-sweet chocolate chips
- 2 teaspoons instant espresso powder or instant coffee
- Almond slices, toasted, for garnish
- Parchment paper

Directions
- Preheat the oven to 350° F. Line cookie sheet with parchment paper.
- In small bowl, combine flour, baking soda, salt, set aside.
- In large bowl, beat butter, sugars, vanilla extract, almond extract until creamy. Add eggs one at a time, beating well after each addition. Gradually beat in flour mixture. Stir in chocolate chips.
- Roll cookies into small balls, place on cookie sheet, bake 10-12 minutes or until golden brown. Transfer to wire racks, cool on cookie sheet for 2 minutes.

For Espresso Ganache:

- In small saucepan, add heavy cream, espresso powder or instant coffee, stirring until combined. Heat cream until it bubbles slightly, turn heat to low. Add chocolate chips, stirring constantly until chocolate is melted completely.
- Cool ganache in refrigerator until thick but spreadable. If too thick, let sit out until softened to desired consistency. Frost cooled cookies with ganache, garnish with almond slices.

Blueberry Streusel Pie
by Hedy Kunstman, friend of Delaware Valley Opera

Ingredients

For pie:

- 3 cup blueberries or huckleberries, fresh or frozen
- ¼ cup sugar
- ¼ cup flour
- 1-2 tablespoon fresh lime juice, or lemon
- 10 inch graham cracker pie crust

Directions

- Preheat oven to 350°F. Mix together all ingredients. Pour mixture into pie crust.

For streusel:

- ¾ cup dark brown sugar
- ½ cup flour
- ½ cup butter, cold, cut in tiny pieces

Directions

- Preheat oven to 350°F. Mix together and shred mixture using two sharp knives or pastry blender until crumbly. Sprinkle streusel on top of berry mixture.
- Bake 10 minutes, reduce heat to 325°F, continue baking another 50 minutes. Serve warm or cold.

Helpful Hints

- Make the streusel ahead of time, keep covered in fridge. If using frozen berries, watch near end of baking time to be sure the pie is bubbly in the middle. If not continue baking until bubbly another 5 minutes or so.

Chocolate Gateau
by Evelyn Franz
from Sylvia Volk

Evelyn Franz is a genius when it comes to creating chocolate desserts. For nearly 30 years she has been the mastermind behind the elegant and delicious desserts at Papa Haydn, a restaurant she co-founded in Portland, Oregon. She first tasted this cake in London at the River Café. They called it "Chocolate Nemesis" and it was love at first bite. When she returned home, Franz developed a recipe for her own rendition.

Ingredients

- 12 ounces dark chocolate, chopped
- ⅓ cup warm espresso or strong coffee
- 4 large eggs, room temperature
- 2 large egg yolks, room temperature
- ¼ cup granulated sugar
- ½ cup heavy whipping cream
- Whipped heavy cream, lightly sweetened, for serving
- Pinch of salt

Directions

- Preheat oven to 350°F degrees. Lightly butter bottom, sides of 8 inch round cake pan, line bottom with parchment paper. Prepare water bath for cake, place washcloth in bottom of medium size roasting pan.
- In large heatproof bowl add chocolate, espresso.

- Set in wide pan of hot water for 5 minutes, stirring 4-5 times until chocolate melts completely. Stir until smooth, keep warm.
- With hand mixer, whip cream until soft peaks form. Set aside.
- Place medium size bowl in hot, 150°F-155°F, water bath. Add eggs, yolks, sugar, salt. With hand mixer, beat until warm, sugar is dissolved. Whisk mixture on high speed until light, fluffy, 2-3 minutes.
- Fold ⅓ of egg mixture and ⅓ whipped cream into chocolate mixture until combined. Pour batter into prepared cake pan, place pan on washcloth in roasting pan, fill roasting pan with hot water halfway up sides of cake pan.
- Bake until top of cake is set, 80-90 minutes. Remove cake from water bath, let cool on wire rack for 30 minutes. Gently loosen edges with thin knife, invert on cooling rack. When cool, carefully remove parchment paper, refrigerate at least 2 hours.

Serve
Slice into thin wedges, serve with whipped cream.

Lemon Curd Opera Cake with Chocolate Buttercream
by Sylvia Volk

This recipe was adapted using less sugar and butter. Silken white chocolate buttercream frosts yellow cake layered with rich lemon curd in this low-sugar version.

Ingredients
For Cake:
- 1 cup (2 sticks) unsalted butter, softened, plus more for pans
- 2½ cup cake flour, sifted, plus more for pans
- 2½ teaspoons baking powder

- 1 teaspoon kosher salt
- ½ cup milk
- 1 teaspoon vanilla extract
- ¾ cup sugar
- 1 tablespoon lemon zest, plus 2 tablespoons juice
- 4 eggs

For curd:
- ¼ cup sugar
- 1 tablespoon lemon zest, plus ⅓ cup juice
- 3 eggs
- 7 tablespoon unsalted butter, cubed, chilled

For buttercream frosting:
- ½ cup sugar
- 3 egg whites
- 1 cup (2 sticks), plus 4 tablespoons unsalted butter, softened
- 2 ounce white chocolate, melted, cooled
- 1 teaspoon vanilla extract
- ⅛ teaspoon kosher salt
- ¾ cup graham crackers, finely ground
- lemon slices, candied, optional garnish

Directions

For cake:
- Preheat oven to 350°F. Butter, flour two 9" round cake pans, set aside.
- In medium bowl, whisk flour, baking powder, salt, set aside. In separate medium bowl, whisk milk, vanilla, set aside.
- Cream butter, sugar, lemon zest, lemon juice with electric mixer on medium-high speed until fluffy, about 3 minutes. Add eggs, one at a time, beating well after each addition.
- In large bowl, mixing on low speed, alternately add dry ingredients, wet ingredients. Increasing speed to high

beat until smooth about 5 seconds.

- Divide batter between prepared pans, smooth tops with rubber spatula. Drop pans lightly on a counter to expel large air bubbles.
- Bake until toothpick inserted in middle comes out clean, 25–30 minutes.
- Let cakes cool 20 minutes in pans, invert onto wire racks, let cool to room temperature.
- Using a serrated knife, halve each cake horizontally to produce four layers.

Directions
For curd:

- In medium saucepan, whisk sugar, lemon zest, juice, eggs until smooth. Cook over medium heat, stirring, until mixture thickens to consistency of loose pudding, about 10 minutes.
- Remove from heat, slowly whisk in butter until melted, smooth. Pour curd through a fine-mesh strainer into bowl. Chill until ready to use.

Directions
For buttercream:

- Place sugar, egg whites in bowl of stand mixer, set over saucepan of simmering water, stir mixture until egg whites register 140°F on an instant-read thermometer. Remove bowl from saucepan and place on stand mixer fitted with a whisk.
- Beat on high speed until meringue is cooled and stiff peaks form. Replace whisk with paddle, add softened butter to meringue; beat until smooth. Stir in white chocolate, vanilla, salt.

To assemble:

- Place one cake layer on cake stand, spread with ⅓ cup curd, repeat with remaining layers and curd, ending with cake layer. Cover top, sides with ¾ of buttercream.

- Place remaining buttercream in pastry bag with plain ½ inch tip, pipe 1 inch mounds along top edge of cake.
- Mix graham crackers, 4 tablespoons melted butter in a bowl and sprinkle along bottom edge of cake.
- Garnish the top of the cake with candied lemon slices, recipe follows.
- Chill cake to firm frosting.

Serve

At room temperature.

Candied Lemon Slices

Ingredients
- 2 lemons, sliced, ⅛ inch thick
- ¼ sugar

Directions
- Preheat the oven to 275°F. Cover baking sheet with parchment paper. Place lemon slices in single layer on parchment, sprinkle ¼ cup granulated sugar over lemon slices.
- Bake 50-60 minutes or until nearly dried and candy glaze hardens. Remove from oven, use a butter knife to gently loosen from parchment, allow to cool. Store in airtight container to prolong shelf life.

Helpful Hint

For a thicker candy coating, in small saucepan mix ¼ cup sugar, ¼ cup water, 1 tablespoon corn syrup. Cook over low heat until sugar dissolves, then bring to boil for approximately 2 minutes. Pour over lemon slices.

Opera Blondies
by Ruth Newman

Ingredients
- ½ cup butter, extra for pan
- 1 cup sugar

- 1 egg, beaten
- ¾ cup flour, sifted
- 1 teaspoon baking powder
- ½ teaspoon vanilla
- 1 tablespoon cocoa
- ½ cup walnuts, optional

Directions

- Preheat oven to 350°F. Prepare 8x8 pan with butter to prevent sticking.
- In medium saucepan, melt butter.
- In large mixing bowl, add butter, sugar, vanilla, egg, flour, baking powder, cocoa, walnuts.
- Bake for 30 minutes, remove when knife inserted comes out clean. Cool on wire rack.

Opera Cake

History

Opera cake is a French type of cake invented by Cyriaque Gavillon from Dalloyau, a Paris based patisserie house dating back to 1682 and the Versailles Court. Gavillon wanted to create a new cake shape with visible layers and for which "only one bite would give the whole cakes taste."

L'Opera made its grand debut in the early 1900s in Paris at the Exposition Culinaire. It was introduced by Louis Clichy, which is why the cake may be referred to as Gâteau Clichy. Many years later the cake was reintroduced as "L'Opera" after the Paris Grand Opera and it became immortal.

Made with layers of almond sponge cake known as Joconde in French, soaked in coffee syrup, layered with ganache and coffee buttercream and covered in chocolate glaze. It is said the name 'opera cake' is perfect as the cake is comprised of several layers, similar to 'acts' in an opera.

Opera Cake for a Busy Soprano
by Danielle DiStefano

Ingredients

- 1 Classic white cake mix
- 1 cup whole milk
- ½ cup (1 stick) melted butter
- 4 whole eggs
- 2-3 teaspoon vanilla extract
- 3-4 teaspoon almond extract

For Espresso Simple Syrup:

- ½ cup water
- ½ cup granulated sugar
- 1 tablespoon instant espresso powder or instant coffee

Espresso Buttercream:

- 1 cup (2 sticks) butter, softened
- 4 cups confectioners sugar, sifted
- 1½ teaspoon vanilla extract
- 2-3 tablespoon whole milk
- 4 tablespoon instant espresso powder or instant coffee

Ganache:

- 2 cups heavy cream
- 2 cups semi-sweet chocolate chips
- Pinch of salt
- Parchment paper
- Soft butter for greasing pan

Directions

For Cake:

- Preheat oven to 350°F. Place 13x9 pan on parchment paper, trace outside of pan with pencil, cut. Coat inside of pan with a little softened butter, place the parchment paper in buttered pan, top with a little softened butter.
- In large bowl, blend cake mix, milk, butter, eggs until just moistened about 30 seconds. Add extracts, beat at medium speed for 2 minutes. Pour into pan, bake 25-30

minutes until toothpick inserted in center comes out with a few crumbs. Cool in pan on wire rack for 15 minutes.

For Simple Syrup:
- In small saucepan, combine water, sugar, espresso powder. Bring to boil over medium heat, stirring until sugar is dissolved. Lower heat, simmer for 3 minutes. Let cool, set aside.

For Espresso Buttercream:
- In large bowl, beat butter until light, fluffy, about 3 minutes.
- In small bowl, combine espresso powder with milk, set aside.
- To large bowl, gradually add powdered sugar 1 cup at a time, alternating with milk mixture, beating well on medium speed. Use discretion when adding milk, keeping the consistency of thick frosting as it will loosen after adding vanilla. Scrape down sides and bottom of bowl. Add vanilla, blend.

To Assemble the Cake:
- Run knife around edges of cooled cake to loosen, flip onto serving platter. With sharp knife, cut cake in half lengthwise, carefully set top half aside on parchment paper.
- Brush bottom half of cake with coffee syrup, spread buttercream. Place top half of cake on top of buttercream, frost cake with ganache.
- Refrigerate 1-3 hours to set. Serve slightly chilled.

Nellie Melba
19 May 1861- 23 February 1931

Dame Nellie Melba, born Helen Porter Mitchell, was an Australian operatic soprano. She became one of the most famous singers of the late Victorian era and early 20th century. She was the first Australian to achieve international recognition as a classical musician. She took the pseudonym "Melba" from Melbourne, her home town. Melba studied singing in Melbourne and made a modest success in performances there.

After a brief and unsuccessful marriage she moved to Europe in search of a singing career. Failing to find engagements in London in 1886 she studied in Paris and soon made a great success there and in Brussels. Returning to London in 1888 she established herself as the leading lyric soprano at Covent Garden.

She soon achieved further success in Paris and elsewhere in Europe and later at the Metropolitan Opera in New York debuting there in 1893. Her repertoire was small; in her whole career she sang no more than 25 roles and was closely identified with only ten. She was known for her performances in French and Italian opera, but sang little German opera.

In 1892, performing in Wagner's opera Lohengrin at Covent Garden, the Duke of Orléans gave a dinner party to celebrate her triumph. For the occasion, Escoffier created a new dessert and to display it, he used an ice sculpture of a swan which is featured in the opera. The swan carried peaches which rested on a bed of vanilla ice cream and topped with spun sugar.

In 1900 Escoffier created a new version of the dessert.

For the occasion of the opening of the Carlton Hotel, where he was head chef, Escoffier omitted the ice swan and topped the peaches with raspberry purée.

Peach Melba
from Sylvia Volk

Ingredients
- 6 peaches, ripe, tender
- 1½ pints vanilla ice cream
- 1 cup raspberries
- 1 cup powdered sugar
- ½ cup sugar
- 6 tablespoons almonds, blanched raw slivers, optional
- Lemon juice, optional

Directions
- Boil medium pot of water. Keep large bowl of ice water close by. Gently submerge a peach into boiling water, simmer for 15-20 seconds. Remove peach from boiling water with slotted spoon, immediately plunge into ice water for a few seconds to cool. Take the peach out of the ice water, place on a plate, repeat process for remaining peaches.
- Peel, discard skins, slice in halve, discard pits.
- In single layer, sprinkle peach halves with sugar on all exposed surfaces. Chill in refrigerator for 1 hour.

Helpful Hint
- The skin should come off easily with short boiling process.

Optional Step
- To keep the peaches from oxidizing and turning brown, place peeled peaches in large bowl of cold water, add 1 tablespoon lemon juice, soak for 10 minutes. Drain water, gently pat dry with paper towel.

For raspberry purée:
- Pulse raspberries in blender a few seconds to create purée, strain in bowl through fine-mesh sieve. With metal spoon, press down extracting as much syrupy juice until only seeds and pulp is left. Dispose of solids or use for smoothies.
- Sift powdered sugar slowly into raspberry purée, alternating whisking until fully incorporated. Refrigerate 1 hour until chilled.

Serve

In six serving dishes, scoop ½ cup vanilla ice cream into each. Place two sugared peach halves on top, drizzle raspberry sauce over peaches and ice cream. Top each with tablespoon of raw almond slivers, if desired. Serve immediately.

Sarah Bernhardt Cookies
by Sylvia Volk

Originating in Denmark and named after the famous French actress who visited Copenhagen in the early 20th century, these decadent almond meringue cookies are topped with chocolate buttercream and dipped in chocolate.

Ingredients
- 8 ounce almonds, whole blanched
- 1½ cup confectioners sugar
- 4 egg whites
- 8 egg yolks
- ½ cup granulated sugar
- 2 cup unsalted butter, softened
- 4 tablespoons cocoa powder
- 16 ounce semi-sweet chocolate

Directions
- Heat oven to 350°F. Line two baking sheets with

parchment paper, set aside. Finely grind almonds in food processor for 1 minute, add confectioners' sugar, mix for 2 minutes. Scrape bottom, insides of bowl to loosen clumps, continue to mix for 3 minutes until very finely ground, set aside.

- Whisk egg whites in standing mixer on medium-low speed until frothy about 2 minutes.
- Increase speed to medium-high, beat until stiff, glossy peaks form about 3 minutes. Transfer whites to a large bowl. Fold in almond mixture in thirds.
- Transfer to large pastry bag fitted with a ½ inch plain pastry tip. Pipe 1 inch rounds about ½ inch apart on baking sheets. Set aside for 10–12 minutes. Bake 15–18 minutes, until stiff. Leave to cool.
- Combine granulated sugar, ¾ cups water in a medium saucepan over medium high. Heat until a thermometer reaches 242°F, about 20 mins.
- Meanwhile, in medium bowl, whisk egg yolks with hand mixer, slowly add sugar syrup, butter, cocoa powder. Mound 1 tablespoon to the bottom of buttercream onto each meringue. Freeze 15 minutes.
- In medium saucepan, pour 1 inch of water, bring to boil, reduce heat to low.
- In medium bowl, add chocolate, place bowl over saucepan. Cook, stirring, until melted and smooth about 5 minutes. Remove from heat, set aside.
- Dip cookies, buttercream side only, in chocolate to fully coat. Place meringue side down on baking sheet, refrigerate until chocolate has hardened.

Swedish Almond Thumbprint Opera Cookies
by Marie Rose, Austin Opera Guild

Ingredients

- ⅔ cup sugar
- 1 cup butter, softened
- ½ teaspoon almond extract
- 2 cups all-purpose flour
- ½ cup jelly or jam

Directions

- Preheat oven to 350°F.
- In large bowl, beat sugar, butter, almond extract at medium speed until creamy. Add flour, reduce speed to low, beat until well mixed. Cover, refrigerate 1 hour.
- Shape dough into 1-inch balls. Place 2 inches apart on cookie sheets.
- With thumb, make indentation in center of each cookie, edges may crack slightly. Fill each indentation with ¼ teaspoon of jelly. Bake 14-18 minutes or until edges are slightly brown.
- Let stand for a couple of minutes. Remove from cookie sheet.

Helpful Hint

To get a variety of flavors and colors, use different jellies, grape, strawberry, apricot, orange marmalade.

The Opera Cocktail

The Opera Cocktail
from Sylvia Volk

Bellini

The Bellini was invented sometime between 1934 and 1948 by Giuseppe Cipriani founder of Harry's Bar in Venice, Italy. Its unique pink color reminded Cipriani of the color of the toga of a saint in a painting by 15th-century Venetian artist Giovanni Bellini. The drink started as a seasonal specialty at Harry's Bar, a favorite haunt of Ernest Hemingway, Sinclair Lewis and Orson Welles. Later it also became popular at the bar's New York counterpart.

The Bellini consists of puréed white peaches and Prosecco, an Italian sparkling wine. Marinating fresh peaches in wine is an Italian tradition. The original recipe was made with a bit of raspberry or cherry juice to give the drink a pink glow. After an entrepreneurial Frenchman set up a business to ship fresh white peach pureé to both locations it was a year-round favorite.

Other sparkling wines are commonly used in place of Prosecco, though richly flavored French champagne does not pair well with the light, fruity flavor of the Bellini. It was an important aspect of celebration in post World War Italy.

California produces a white peach that works well, yellow peaches or peach nectar can be substituted. Other fruits or even flavored liqueurs, peach schnapps for example, are sometimes substituted for the peach puree. For a non-alcoholic version, sparkling juice or seltzer is used in place of the champagne.

Fresh Peach & Raspberry Bellini

Ingredients
- Champagne
- Peaches, fresh or frozen, remove skin, pits cut in chunks
- Raspberries, fresh or frozen
- Sugar, fine

Directions
- Remove skins, pits from peaches, cut into chunks. Add to blender, blend on medium speed until pureed. Add raspberries, sugar, blend together on medium speed.

Serve
- In tall champagne flutes, add 2 or 3 tablespoons puree, fill with chilled champagne.

Strawberry Bellini

Ingredients
- 6 strawberries, sliced
- ¼ cup powdered sugar
- 2 tablespoons brandy
- 3 cups Prosecco or sparkling wine

Directions
In blender, mix strawberries, sugar, brandy until smooth. Let stand for 10 minutes, chill.

Serve
Add ¼ cup strawberry mixture to 4 champagne glasses. Add Prosecco, garnish with strawberry.

Bellini Schnapps

Dip rims of champagne glasses in fine sugar. Add one ounce peach schnapps, fill with chilled champagne.

About The Authors

Wayne Line

Baritone Wayne Line has sung in China, Bulgaria, The Czech Republic, Germany, Austria, Canada and the United States. He has performed in the Canadian premier of The Ballad of Baby Doe, as Horace Tabor for Opera in the Ozarks, as Germont in La Traviata, for the Natchez Festival of Music as Michele in Il Tabarro, Lazar Wolf in Fiddler on the Roof and as the District Attorney in the world premiere of SHOT! with Nickel City Opera.

Mr.Line has performed major roles for Summer Opera Lyric Theater, Viva Musica in Canada, the Societa dei concerti di Santa Margherita in Italy, South Florida Opera and Delaware Valley Opera including Falstaff in The Merry Wives of Windsor, Peter in Hansel and Gretel, Conte di Luna in Il Trovatore, Gaylord Ravenal in Showboat, Marcello in La Boheme and Count Almaviva in Le Nozze di Figaro. He has recently expanded his experience to include stage directing at Delaware Valley Opera.

In Die Fledermaus, Mr. Line's *"robust voice was well-articulated and well-projected, his acting fluid and dramatic."*

...Opera Canada

Sylvia Volk

Sylvia was a co-founder of OperaBuffs of Western New York promoting opera to its members through newsletters, lectures, trips and events welcoming everyone. Through her work with the Greater Buffalo Opera Company (GBOC) she tirelessly campaigned to make opera visible in the Western New York community and was the original editor of the WNY Vocal Alert. When she lived in Oregon, she started an opera lecture series held at the library in her new community. Before her death Sylvia spoke of the opera cookbook that she and Eileen were developing. She would be so happy to know that the cookbook has finally come to fruition.

Eileen Breen

In 2009 Eileen started Nickel City Opera with Metropolitan Opera Singer, Valerian Ruminski, now in its 11th Season. Wearing many hats, she wrote and secured the 501(c)3 non profit status, is a successful grant writer and provides full service public relations and marketing campaign for a variety of clients. From creating innovative, fundraising events and effective sponsorship campaigns to negotiating theatrical contracts, "it can't be done" is not a part of her vocabulary.

Sharing her time and expertise, Eileen has volunteered with numerous non profit organizations including The New York Musical Theatre Festival, The NYC Fringe Festival and NYC Dance Week in addition to teaching a popular class, 'The Media Truth' at the International Center in NYC.

43239779R00104

Made in the USA
Middletown, DE
22 April 2019